POSTGRADUATE RESEARCH IN BUSINESS

Dedication

This book is dedicated to the memory of Stuart Rooks who inspired and enormously encouraged us in our teaching and writing. It is also for our children Edmund, Olivia, Aidan and Ella with love.

POSTGRADUATE RESEARCH IN BUSINESS A Critical Guide

Sarah Quinton and Teresa Smallbone

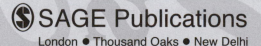

SAGE Publications

London • Thousand Oaks • New Delhi

SAGE Publications Ltd
1 Oliver's Yard
55 City Road
London EC1Y 1SP

SAGE Publications Inc.
2455 Teller Road
Thousand Oaks, California 91320

SAGE Publications India Pvt Ltd
B-42, Panchsheel Enclave
Post Box 4109
New Delhi 110 017

British Library Cataloguing in Publication data

A catalogue record for this book is available
from the British Library

ISBN-10 1-4129-0835-3   ISBN-13 978-1-4129-0835-1
ISBN-10 1-4129-0836-1   ISBN-13 978-1-4129-0836-8 (pbk)

Library of Congress Control Number: 2005931794

Typeset by C&M Digitals (P) Ltd., Chennai, India
Printed in Great Britain by The Cromwell Press Ltd, Trowbridge, Wiltshire
Printed on paper from sustainable resources

Contents

Acknowledgements   vi

About this Book   vii

1   What is Management Research and What Does it mean at Masters' Level?   1

2   Developing a Critical Approach   15

3   Generating, Developing and Mapping Ideas for Research Topics   28

4   Making your Project Manageable   44

5   Sources of Secondary Information   67

6   How to Read Critically   81

7   Organizing and Analysing What You Have Read and Researched   97

8   Reflection – How to Learn to Be a Better Researcher and Business Manager from Doing Research   110

9   Reliability, Validity and Generalization   125

10   Writing Up and Beyond   141

References   162

Index   167

Acknowledgements

We would like to thank the many people who have helped us in writing this book, in particular, our editor Patrick Brindle for his patience and support, and our colleagues at Oxford Brookes Business School, especially Sally Harridge-March and Jackie Clarke. Emma Coles from the Business School resource centre provided invaluable help with the production of the manuscript and the design of the artwork. Niall O' Dochartaigh gave us permission to use his work on the reliability of internet sources and we are grateful to him. We would also like to thank Chris Blackburn and Mark Saunders for their encouragement to write this book and our many students, particularly on the Oxford Brookes MSc in International Management and the Named Awards, who have contributed to our learning about what makes a good researcher. Chris Peach and Janis Millers, both former students, have allowed us to use some of their work.

About this Book

Who Is It For?

This book is for all Masters' students, including MBA and DMS students, in business and business-related subjects, who are about to embark on some research or to write a dissertation. We also think that PhD students will find a lot of it very helpful. Supervisors of research may also find it a useful tool for helping their students to unravel the mysteries of research.

The book is the culmination of many years' experience of teaching and supervising business and management students. It includes much material that we have developed as teaching aids to help communicate the concept of 'good' research and the processes required to make research 'good'. We discovered while teaching research methods and supervising dissertations that many textbooks offer guidance on research, but that they assume a level of knowledge and use terminology that is really intimidating to novice researchers. The aim of this book is to support you, the researcher, in thinking about, creating, developing, researching and writing up your research project or dissertation successfully. Becoming an active researcher can be rather like becoming a member of a club where there is an unwritten code of how members should dress and behave. This book offers you the key to that 'members' information.

What Does It Do?

This is a practical 'how to' guide – we tell you what you need to know in order to pass your dissertation. Not only is there practical advice, but we also offer some of the academic theory you will need. You can find plenty of help in the research methods textbooks on how to write a questionnaire or run a focus group and so these aspects of data collection are not covered here. Instead, we concentrate on how you can make sure that you can demonstrate that you have come up with the right sort of topic, read the right academic literature 'critically', reflected on the research process and met the many other assessment criteria demanded of Masters'-level business students.

The book tells you how to get started on your project and what you need to know in order to pitch it at the right level – and how to find ideas for what is probably going to be the biggest single piece of academic work you will ever do. It provides a map to help you think about and carry out good quality management research. It guides you through the process of finding ideas for research topics, particularly with dissertations in mind. It suggests useful tools and techniques for making your research project manageable and achievable, and helps you to find a means of tracking down, assessing and evaluating information, drawing valid conclusions from it and writing it up. We aim to enable you to bridge the gap between theory and practice, so that you are able to show that you are aware that there are a variety of approaches to the construction of knowledge, even if you then choose to follow one particular path.

How to Use this Book

This book is not intended to replace the many established research methods textbooks; rather we feel that it should be used as a core component of your reading to help you tackle the difficult issues – meeting the requirements of your course and examiners as well as delivering satisfying and useful research outcomes. You can access the more specialized books in your institution's library to find out about specific tools and techniques. The book can be read from cover to cover, but it will be equally beneficial to you if you read chapters as and when you need them. You will find discussion questions and suggested further reading at the end of each chapter, use these to consolidate your knowledge and improve your research skills.

Chapters 1 and 2 help you to understand what exactly management research is all about and make you aware of current debates in both the academic and the business world about the nature and relevance of research in this area. They then go on to help you to understand why, in order to satisfy the academic requirements of a Masters' degree, you have to develop a critical approach to the subject and how you can go about it. Chapter 3 offers lots of practical help in finding and developing good ideas for dissertation and research projects that will meet the requirements of your university or college and sustain your interest and enthusiasm. In Chapter 4, we help you with establishing boundaries to your research, so you know how much you need to do and so you can make sure that your project is feasible and realistic. We also help you turn your topic ideas into achievable research objectives, questions and hypotheses. In Chapter 5, we help you to identify what is the most appropriate literature for your assignments and dissertations by looking at the vast range of secondary information that is available and giving you a guide to what is worth including. We suggest good ways of showing that you have met the academic requirement of using a 'wide range' of secondary data.

In Chapter 6, we show you how to become critical readers of typical academic literature in business and management, a key requirement of postgraduate education. Although the focus is on developing your skills at reading academic journal articles, this skill needs to be developed for all your work. Chapter 7 offers practical advice on how to organize your burgeoning collection of notes and data, how to record and store material and how to start sorting and coding raw data. In Chapter 8, we help you to learn to reflect – to make sure that you are actually learning from doing your research to become a better researcher and a better manager with a consistent approach to tackling and leaning from problems and experience. Chapter 9 returns to more academic issues that are essential for passing and getting good marks in your work – making sure that your research is reliable and valid and helping you to decide where you can generalize from it to other situations or populations. In Chapter 10, we provide practical advice on how to write up your research. This includes a consideration of who you are writing for – your audience – and how to plan your dissertation; we also suggest a possible structure for your work and discuss how to present an effective argument.

1 What is Management Research and What Does it Mean at Masters' Level?

What Have I Got to Do?

This chapter starts by discussing what exactly the purpose and focus of management research is; which is not as obvious as it might at first seem. The aim is to provide a context for what follows in the succeeding chapters. It provides a guide to what various leading academics think about their subject, explains why it is a topic of debate and provides some background to what you will be learning on your Masters' or diploma course. It identifies the potentially significant contributions that can be made by Masters' students to management knowledge through carrying out research projects, and discusses the need for a critical approach in all management research and thinking.

The rest of this book guides you through the process of finding ideas for research topics, particularly with dissertations in mind. It suggests useful tools and techniques for making your research project manageable and achievable, and helps you to find a means of tracking down, assessing and evaluating information, drawing valid conclusions from it and writing it up.

What is Management Research?

As part of your Masters' degree or diploma, you will be expected to undertake some research into business and management. Before you start, you need to know what exactly constitutes 'research' in business and management and why it is worth doing. More than 85 universities and colleges in the UK teach management as a degree level subject (McLaughlin and Thorpe, 2000) and there are, of course, many more worldwide. Most of them also carry out research into the subject. But it is not clear what all this research is for, nor whether it is trying to do something practical – given that management is seen by many people as a practical subject – or whether it is in pursuit of knowledge for its own sake – which is perhaps what academic study is for. In 1994, Burgoyne suggested that there were a number of facets of management learning that arose both from doing research into the subject and from the practical experience of management. In his view, it is an applied philosophy in the sense of applying theory to the solution of practical problems, and research in the subject area should focus on that.

He described management as an 'emerging' area of study that changes all the time, with a focus that is multidisciplinary and that borrows and synthesizes from many academic disciplines, as well as being an area of professional practice (Burgoyne, 1994). The quality of management research was recognized as a problem by the 'Bain Report' in 1994, which suggested that all management research should try to improve the understanding and practice of managers through what they termed 'the double hurdle' of research that is high quality both from the point of view of managers and of researchers. Bain thought academics should develop research on topics that are of critical importance to organizations and managers, and that the users of such research should be committed to academic independence and freedom to publish (McLaughlin and Thorpe, 2000).

In a much quoted article and one that is well worth reading, Tranfield and Starkey in 1998 posed some key questions about the nature and purpose of academic research in business and management. For example, they ask whether management research in universities is primarily for managers? Or is it about them and their organizations? The problem of defining exactly what constitutes management research goes much wider than just this. There is both uncertainty as to its status, a lack of consensus as to how it should be carried out, which can make it difficult to execute, and recognition of the limits of scientific methods and any claims that it is value free. The academic debate about the nature and relevance of management research has continued on both sides of the Atlantic, notably in the pages of the *British Journal of Management*, which devoted a whole special issue to the subject in 2001, and in the US-based *Academy of Management Review*.

Just as more and more students are studying and researching the topic of management at university, out in the workplace management has become more than just a job. Managers are being given a critical role in reshaping society in areas such as reforming the public services. This alone makes it essential that we carry out good quality research into how this is working out in practice. Increasingly, management academics are arguing that management now needs to be supported by a research base that reflects the interests of society as a whole, not just one part of it. For example, in the past, management research has reflected the assumption that management is a white able-bodied male activity (McLaughlin and Thorpe, 2000).

The immense scope and potential role of management research makes it open to criticism from many specific subject areas and the breadth of possibilities of research within it may mean that many topics are only researched at a superficial level. Tranfield and Starkey (1998) applied a framework for exploring the attributes of academic subjects to the whole subject of management. For anyone who reads this thinking that the course they are on will give them access to a coherent body of knowledge and practice that can then be applied in the world of work, be prepared to be disappointed! They characterize management as a soft (in the sense that it is not governed by a body of theory subscribed to by all management researchers, however loosely defined), applied, divergent (as it lacks a unity of purpose), and rural discipline (because there is a wide area of study with no clear demarcation lines and little communication between researchers). They suggest that management's position in the social sciences is similar to the position of engineering in the physical sciences or medicine in biological science. They conclude that management research needs to be 'transdisciplinary', heterogeneous, more socially accountable and to involve collaboration from different disciplines. By 'transdisciplinary', they suggest that management research should be developing its own framework to guide problem solving that is at some level practical, but also has theoretical elements and so will represent a contribution to knowledge. They issue a call for such research to be cross-cultural rather than guided by American experience.

The Management Research Tradition in Business Schools

If you consider very briefly the history of management education at degree level, it is easy to discern a number of phases of management school development. The first MBA was introduced at Harvard University in 1908 (Mintzberg, 2004) and the second one, also in the USA, at Stanford in 1925. Although management has been taught at degree level since the beginning of the 20th century in some countries, it was not until the 1960s that the subject really began to take off on an international scale. Early management departments tended to be heavily US influenced, and to involve disciplines such as engineering, accounting, economics, and behavioural science. Their research base was and is strongly rooted in applied quantitative methods, with a view of research strongly oriented towards the natural sciences. In the 1960s, management researchers tended to adopt a multidisciplinary approach, borrowing from economics and psychology, and from the professions, particularly accountancy and marketing. There was a strong emphasis on effective decision-making, the use of quantitative methods of analysis, and model-building. This approach is sometimes described as normative theories of management and is still dominant in the USA and France. Ehrensal (n.d) argues that in the USA management research focuses on a 'science of administration' so that its aim is to train future managers, and not to critically appraise existing values and systems of management. Mintzberg suggests that the MBA programmes taught in US business schools reduce 'managing to decision-making and decision-making to analysis' (Mintzberg, 2004: 38), with a particular emphasis within that on evaluation of possible choices when decisions are made, as that is the sole area amenable to systematic analysis.

Mintzberg (1973) and many others have criticized this research tradition as unrealistic, because it is not based on observation of what managers actually do and implicitly therefore lacks a sociological perspective. Their approach stresses the need to help managers to do better what they do most of, which is working and negotiating with others, rather than devising and implementing grand strategies. They advocate the use of 'softer' research methods to describe and analyse these modes of working. In the 1980s, management as a subject became more interdisciplinary, with a more open attitude to learning from many research traditions, and a tendency to view it increasingly as an applied behavioural science. One European-based school of thought argues strongly that even this on its own is insufficient, as the interpretation of data is so often unreflective. 'Reflexive understanding', which involves a self-critical look at our own assumptions and perspectives, is in this view essential to carrying out high-quality research in management and business, as is the need to include historical and political research perspectives as an acknowledgement of the dominant tradition.

A third phase of management school development that involves the inclusion of pedagogic strategies to facilitate learning and embracing learning about management for the sake of it, rather than to solve a specific problem, is now underway. The learning processes are seen as being as important as the management tools used to solve the knotty issue for managers that is under study. Management research is a living subject that changes, stretches and grows, so that a circular process whereby theory informs practice that informs theory is seen as the ideal, although Das (2003) would argue that theory does not inform practice, as the former is too far removed from the latter to be of any practical use. However, in the last 10 years or so there has been a collective attempt to redress this, partially through the acceptance and credibility of MBA programmes at renowned higher education institutions, originating in the USA, but now firmly entrenched in Europe.

Why Do People Do Management Research?

There are many reasons why people choose to be active researchers in the management area. There is internal pressure for university departments to be seen to be engaging with research and having a demonstrable research output that can then be fed back into teaching. For purely pragmatic reasons, if you are an academic, it is likely to improve your credibility within your given subject if you have researched and published in the relevant journals or perhaps contributed to a textbook. Your research and subsequent publications will give you some kudos amongst colleagues and could also enhance your academic career aspirations.

Many academics and practitioners also want to improve understanding of their subject. Research within a specific area with the aim of developing understanding about a given management issue is one of the most effective ways of achieving this. The drive to move a subject forwards and the satisfaction from being part of an evolutionary process is what encourages and sustains many researchers. It can be very satisfying to see your recommendations based on your research being put into practice. It is also rewarding for academics to be able to discuss their research with students who may offer useful contributions and criticisms particularly at Masters' level.

External pressure in the form of universities' continuing need for improved funding also acts as a driver for pursuing management research. Successful bids for research projects can improve a university's profile within the education sector and bring much-needed funds into a given university. The rating given to a university following a research evaluation exercise may also make a significant difference to the amount of funding provided for an academic institute.

Where Does Management Research Fit?

Management research uses knowledge and research methods drawn from other disciplines in the social sciences and beyond, though not everyone is even agreed that management itself is a form of applied sociology or applied economics, or even applied psychology. Hatchuel (2001) makes the case for distinguishing management science from the other social sciences. He suggests that it does not study economic or social facts, but what he terms 'models of collective action' springing from its origins as a search by practitioners for solutions to practical problems within firms. This still sounds a bit like sociology, though.

If you look at the qualifications and particularly the first degrees of many management academics, you will find that very many of them did not study the subject at undergraduate level, but came into it as postgraduates. Similarly, management is one of the few subjects you can start at postgraduate level without having studied the subject at all before. This is one of its great strengths, because the people teaching and studying the subject will embody a variety of research traditions and approaches. Your past knowledge and experience in whatever subject area will not be wasted, as management research can be considered inclusive. First degrees in modern languages, engineering or philosophy can provide just as relevant a background and insight as a first degree in business or statistics. Do not discard your knowledge of literary criticism, economic geography, experimental psychology or close textual analysis. The skills developed in studying a huge range of subjects – or in sorting out practical issues in your work – are all highly relevant to management research.

Tranfield and Starkey (1998) and others suggest that one of the most striking things about management research is that it operates from no core theory or agreed paradigm that everyone within the field works to. A paradigm is a pattern or framework that forms our thinking before we even begin our research. It was defined as such by Thomas Kuhn (1962) when he was trying to describe how scientists make break-throughs in knowledge and what the distinction was between creating a new mode of thinking – a new paradigm – or refining or developing an existing one. However, as the section on the tradition of management education outlined above suggests, the dominant research tradition in management has tended in the past to be based on testing theories using quantitative data collection derived largely from asking managers, and others, questions in surveys, the results of which are then subject to extensive statistical testing. This approach is described as deductive (the theory testing) and positivist (the data collection method). There is another approach that has gradually gained acceptance, which seeks to derive theories from the data, and which uses a different approach to data collection that may involve the collection of much more detailed information but from a very few informants. The approach is qualitative, in that you try to get as much data as possible of a much deeper variety. The data is subject to detailed analysis but it is not statistically based. This approach is described as inductive (the theory building) and phenomenological (the data collection method). In reality, there is not such a sharp divide between these two research approaches. There is a continuum leading between the two poles and most researchers find themselves somewhere along it. The actual research tools that you will end up using can be a mixture of qualitative and quantitative methods and parts of the same research project can be inductive while others are deductive.

Unlike in the natural sciences, it is not usually possible to tell what frame of reference or paradigm a management researcher is using when he or she approaches a piece of research, but as a student you may be asked to discuss or to declare what your 'ontological' perspective is in your dissertation. In some business research programmes you may be required to state what your ontological perspective is at the outset, and in order to do this you need to know what your own view of the world is based on. Are you for example drawn to a positivist view of research or is your perspective more phenomenological? Your approach to your research should be guided by what you want to find out. Your choice of a topic to research (see Chapter 3) may lead you into adopting a particular research philosophy, or you may have to be wholly pragmatic and use the tools that are available to you in order to carry out your research and then design a rationale that fits it later.

We believe that good management research stems from the multidisciplinary origins of the subject with the strongest roots coming from the social sciences. For many purposes, it may not even be distinct from other subjects, as it is an amalgamation of several. There is no need to decide at the outset that your research has to be either deductive or inductive or to make value judgments about either type of research; both are possible.

What is Management Theory?

Most postgraduate degrees expect you to make a 'contribution to theory' or to knowledge in the course of your research, and this might be one of the marking criteria for your dissertation. A theory enables you to predict and explain phenomena and it can give you a much better understanding of the data you have collected. It also enables you to make generalizations from the data you have available. The lack of a central paradigm means that it is very difficult to distinguish any core management theory or to work out the role of theory in management research. Management academics are inevitably divided about the role of theory in management research and about what exactly constitutes theory. For example, the resource-based view of the firm has been described as a theory by some authors, but others hotly contest this (see Priem and Butler, 2001 if you want a flavour of this particular debate). Some view concepts such as Porter's five forces model as a theory, whereas we see it as an analytical tool (see Chapter 9 for more on this) that can form a useful framework for organizing some of your data.

It is rather unlikely that you will be able to come up with some grand theory of organizational behaviour in the context of your dissertation, nor will you be expected to. If your research approach tends to be phenomenological, there may not in any case be much distinction in your work between theory and data – the data may throw up new ideas about theory and your explanations or theorizing about that data may change and adapt as you carry out your research. In a wide-ranging article, Llewellyn suggests that there are five levels of theorizing, with the highest level being 'grand theory', but she emphasizes that for many purposes you do not actually need a theory at this high level. What is needed, in her view, is what she calls a conceptual tool that is relevant to a particular problem that you are investigating (Llewellyn, 2003), and this may very well be at the level of a straightforward metaphor or simile, or a theory that is dependant on the context, rather than an all-embracing explanation. In Chapter 3 we suggest that one source of a dissertation topic might be to take a model developed or described in an academic journal article in one context and then to apply it to another, or to test it using a different source of data. In practice, this is what many management academics do in their research, and it is generally accepted as a contribution to knowledge.

A Critical Approach?

The traditional model of management education gives students a very limited, if any, opportunity to challenge the conventional wisdom of authors, models, the North American management perspective or the case studies presented to them. Many international students still hold a desire to be socialized into the ways of western management thinking in order to 'fit in' to an organization and see their postgraduate education, especially the MBA, as a means of achieving this. A critical approach should generate openness to alternative ways of thinking (Currie and Knights, 2003) across subject areas and is not only applicable to management. Management research, in our view, should encourage the acceptance of openness and pluralism, in that there may be several routes to take in a piece of research, many of which may have equal value. The emphasis given by many higher education institutions in promoting the value of doing postgraduate management studies as a means of enhancing your career opportunities, whilst at the same time asking their students to critique and challenge the systems and values of the corporate world they hope to enter, can leave students bewildered. There may be a tendency for teachers to be regarded as management experts by students, who are able and prepared to provide the 'right' answer. We hope that by the time you have finished this book you will know that there is no right answer! If teachers of management encourage their students to adopt a critical approach, they have to be open in not trying to give the 'right' answer and are therefore potentially vulnerable to criticism by those students who expect one. This may result in a classroom and research culture that some students may feel uncomfortable with (Sturdy and Gabriel, 2000). But there is a need to challenge and question in management teaching and research if we are to produce rigorous and innovative managers and researchers. This critical dialogue and critical thinking should be carried forward into the thinking you do about researching and writing up your dissertation.

Critical management research requires an open attitude and an expectation that we do not 'see' the results before they appear. The role of a modern critical researcher is to open the way for discourse rather than to find the 'one true way'. Insight (real understanding), critique (deconstruction) and transformation (real learning) all make up the critical role. You are more likely to be open if you are familiar with a variety of approaches and research strategies, which is why following one method, such as the traditional Harvard Business School approach of case study analysis, where MBA students tackle 500 cases over 2 years, may be very limiting. The trick in writing your dissertation, which is what this book is about, is to try to bridge the gap between theory and practice, and to at least demonstrate that you are aware that there are a variety of approaches to the construction of knowledge, even if you then choose to follow one particular path.

If you delve further into critical management research, you are likely to come across literature on critical theory. Critical management theorists developed their ideas after becoming disillusioned with the established forms of management theory and practice and include authors such as Matts Alvesson and Hugh Willmott, who in turn draw on sociologists such as Horkheimer. Central to their position is the belief that management is a social phenomenon that has such an impact upon so many lives that research into it should not be limited to traditional 'positivist' approaches, but should encompass approaches from other disciplines. A full discussion of critical theory and its application to management studies can be found in Alvesson and Willmott's book published in 1992.

The Practitioners' View

One of the problems with management as a subject of research is that it is so complex. It is very difficult to work out precise measures of cause and effect because the environment is so dynamic and skilful managers use intuition as well as rational analysis, which is very hard to identify and analyse for research purposes. Moreover, the daily reality of managing makes recommendations from academic research appear less significant and of less real value. There is a real tension between academics not valuing practitioner experience and practitioners not recognizing the potential worth of academic management research. In the UK, the success of British industry and services depends upon how organizations use knowledge (Department of Trade and Industry, 1998). Research and theory can enhance the knowledge base from which management decisions are taken. Universities and research institutions are a source of external learning from which an organization can draw. Management decisions can be criticized for a lack of rigour and decisions may be made that are based on a hunch or on sector experience rather than on evidence-based research.

But academic research in business may be of little or no help to practitioners. Das (2003) cites academic research using students as samples as inappropriate to say the least and not worthy of publication. It is undoubtedly the case that academics do need to have some knowledge of the managerial world and the harsh realities of commerce before undertaking any management research if they wish their findings to be seen as credible in the business community. This is why, particularly if you are an MBA or DMS student, your work experience is so potentially valuable.

In a later article, Tranfield et al. (2004) comment that a large proportion of management research is created in academic institutions, while most management decisions are based on experience, intuition, creativity and judgement rather than masses of data. At the same time, a lot of management research is essentially descriptive because it is trying to understand people and processes in organizations. Many potential users of management research believe that it could benefit them, but they want statements of what is best practice and advice they can act on rather than a reflexive analysis of a problem (Starkey and Madan, 2001). There is a need to develop management knowledge and one way to do this is by incorporating academic research. The divide between academic knowledge and its relevance for practitioners is not confined to the subject of management. Tranfield et al. suggest that systematic reviews of published evidence, as has been pioneered in the medical sciences, could be a way of getting research taken up in practice.

Literature looking at how to bridge the divide between management and academic research includes Tranfield et al.'s suggestion of knowledge co-production, which involves collaboration between academics and practitioners (2004). Unfortunately, but perhaps not surprisingly, most organizations will not agree to the publication of research that shows them to be failing to any extent, or that might harm their competitive advantage. There are other problems with putting the ideal of joint academic and practical use into research practice. Several academic authors have noted that there is in practice a huge divide between what academics research in their specialisms and what non-academic stakeholders are interested in. In the field of industrial work and organizational psychology, for example, Hodgkinson et al. (2001) argue that the vast majority of academic studies follow on from other published studies with few aimed at testing theory and even fewer at addressing a relevant issue. They characterize this trend to what they describe as increasing methodological rigour at the expense of relevance as 'pedantic science'. The result is that the majority of published articles in the top journals on issues such as personnel selection and assessment are so technical that few can understand them. A similar situation exists in areas such as finance theory and strategic management (Starkey and Madan, 2001). In marketing, leading American journals such as the *Journal of Marketing* and the *Journal of Consumer Research* regularly carried articles by practitioners in the 1950s and 1960s, but it is almost inconceivable that they would do so today (Brown, 1995), and marketing scholarship has become increasingly divorced from practice. Users of management research only need enough methodological rigour to ensure that the evidence on which they will base their decisions has itself a sound basis. At the other end of the spectrum, there is a vast array of populist management books that have very little theoretical basis or methodological rigour, but sell well in airport bookstalls, and are undoubtedly far more widely read by practising managers than the leading academic journals.

The style of research writing often alienates managers (Kelemen and Bansal, 2002), and the length of articles also puts off casual readers. Much academic research is written without a specific audience in mind beyond the stylistic requirements of the journal the article is submitted to, which also has the effect of severely limiting the size of the potential audience. Even the place of publication means that it is frequently hard to find it outside the academic environment and academic database subscriptions (Willmott, 1994). If academic management research output were presented in a different style, and in one that engaged managers, then practitioners would pay more attention to their research output (Kelemen and Bansal, 2002).

What Do We Expect from Management Research?

As managers, perhaps the answer to this question is 'very little' (see above the comments by authors such as Das who have crossed and re-crossed the divide between practitioner and manager.) Do we expect the resolution of a specific work problem or issue? Do managers wish to see detailed and actionable recommendations at the end of pieces of research? Do managers even value academic research in management? If, as many might argue, research increases knowledge about a subject, then it would seem logical that managers would welcome academics' research output. However, if managers cannot make any concrete use of this research (Keleman and Bansal, 2002), or find it irrelevant (Astley and Zummuto, 1992), they are less likely to support it. None the less, this does not mean that discursive or conceptual research should be abandoned, but perhaps that it should be presented to practitioners in a different manner in order to gain acceptance.

As researchers we might expect management research to be treated with more reverence than it currently is. We would all like to feel as individual researchers that we are making valuable contributions to the subject area. In truth, very little management research filters its way into management practice, but the research may well have significant value in teaching not only about management but also about rigour and depth of thought. We should stop looking at the tensions and start looking at the potential for mutually beneficial co-existence; can we aim to better understand each other's worlds?

Where Do I Fit In as a Masters' Student and What Contribution Should I be Making?

At postgraduate level for students with practical business experience, a Masters' degree, such as the DMS or MBA, offers the opportunity for you to explore whether the theory you are taught fits your actual experience. In addition, as someone with a practitioner view, a Masters' degree can give you insight into different approaches that you might take in the future when faced with making a management decision. As a Masters' student with experience, you can reflect on your own performance and abilities when dealing with work situations. Thus, for a student who has been in the workplace, a Masters' degree in business and management offers the chance to put your work into a wider context.

As a Masters' student without any substantial management experience, you are likely to be studying for an MSc or MA. You may have chosen to continue studying immediately after your undergraduate degree and so be used to writing and thinking about theoretical concepts. Studying business and management at Masters' level will allow you to explore concepts and possibly test them out using primary research. Whichever route you come from, you will be using your critical faculties to appraise previous research and make important judgements about theory and practice in business and management. Do not underrate your potential contribution to the subject area.

You may end up conducting research that is original, that looks at a management area from a different perspective, or perhaps helps to fill a gap in the knowledge about a sector or business culture in a certain country. Your work may inform the 'scholarship' in a given topic and may be published as an illustrative case study or be presented as a conference paper at a national-level conference. Business and management teachers draw on such material to use in their teaching, which in turn helps future managers to learn. Therefore, Masters' students can add significant value to the subject. As a Masters' student you may end up so interested and motivated by your subject that you may decide to take a PhD or professional qualification and continue to research and then to integrate your research findings into management activity. This may appear a foolish notion at the moment, but do not discard the idea, as many Masters' students have done exactly that.

Opportunities for Research in Business and Management

There are opportunities to develop research in all areas of management, but Bessant et al. (2003) in the *British Journal of Management* recently highlighted the following areas as rather thinly represented in the management research output. If you think you might want to make a career in management research, or you feel inspired to look at areas where there has not been a great deal of prior research, you might wish to consider these as potential topic areas for your own research at Masters' level. They include research into small and medium sized enterprises (SMEs) and entrepreneurship generally. There is a relatively small body of work published, which largely consists of illustrative examples used as case studies of successes or failures of small and start-up companies. The area of finance in business is growing in importance, but needs further work, as does information systems. The applications of both of these in business and management need to be researched further. The authors, who sat on the panel that rated all the research done in British universities in the Research Assessment Exercise in 2001, believe that a more rigorous approach to marketing research is required, which would thus strengthen the credibility of the subject. The use of tools to evaluate marketing activity and a critique of these is just one example of a research opportunity. Tourism research could be enhanced and expanded by linking it more explicitly to management and operations rather than the consumer experience (Bessant et al., 2003).

Where Do I Go from Here?

Having read this far, you may now be thinking – what do I do next?

It may prove useful to ask yourself the questions below.

Are there any constraints concerning my research strategy or research tools?

If you are an MBA or DMS student, you may have little or no choice over this. For example, if you are conducting research as part of a larger ongoing company research project, it may be in a particular form over which you have no control. Likewise, it may be a condition of access to a company that you research a specific area using specific tools, though you may have a greater influence on how it is executed and analysed. If you are sponsored and still an employee of the business, you need to comply fully with any constraints imposed in order not to jeopardize your position.

If you are an MSc or MA student, the strategy you choose to adopt will influence your choice of data collection tools. It is not advisable to start by thinking that you will use a questionnaire and work backwards; it may very well be the wrong tool to use to provide data that will answer your research objectives when analysed. You need to think about your whole approach to your research and what your overarching strategy is before determining the relevant data collection tools.

Which perspective will I take?

Although the word limits set by your examining institution may vary from 12 000 to 20 000 words, you will not be able to focus on both the organization and the individual or the organization and the consumer in your management research. Trying to cover both very different perspectives will not allow you to develop the sufficient depth that is required at Masters' level. You must decide which perspective to focus on. For example, are you exploring consumer buying behaviour as it relates to branded goods or are you exploring corporate brand identity? Even though both angles are about brands and issues of brand management, you cannot expect to cover both in one dissertation. It may be helpful to split business and management research into the following four perspectives to help you find a focus: the organization itself; the employees and internal issues; channel members; and, finally, the end user and consumer.

Summary

This chapter introduced and discussed the nature and complexities of management research. It outlined the differing and evolving management research traditions in business schools in Europe and America. It discussed the practitioner's view of management research and why people engage in it. The contribution that can be made by Masters' students has been highlighted, as has the need for a critical approach in all management research and thinking.

Discussion Questions

1 As a potential researcher of management, where is your starting position?

2 What do you think may be the value of researching into management topics?

3 As a manager what would you wish to be the outcome of a piece of academic research into your area?

Further Reading

Easterby-Smith, M., Thorpe, R. and Lowe, A. (2002) *Management Research: An Introduction.* **London: Sage.** A readable and interesting introduction to the whole subject.

Gummesson, E. (2000) *Qualitative Methods in Management Research* **(2nd edition). Thousand Oaks, CA: Sage Publications.** Well worth reading, as it looks at management research from the perspective of someone who is trying to do it and the practical issues they face.

2 Developing a Critical Approach

What Does it Mean to be 'Critical' in an Academic Context?

The aim of this chapter is to provide an insight into what academics mean when they require you to be 'critical' in your thinking, reading and writing and to explain why it matters in management and business research at Masters' level. This chapter discusses the need for a critical approach to your work and why it is so important for your degree.

What is a 'Critical' Approach and Why Does it Matter?

At Masters' level, you are supposed to demonstrate 'a critical approach' to your tutors, examiners and even your peers, but what exactly is it and how do you become 'critical' in your approach? Course requirements and marking guides are peppered with requirements to 'show evidence of a critical approach to material' or 'critical understanding', and so forth, but many people are unsure what academics mean by this and may be afraid to ask for fear of looking foolish (Poulson and Wallace, 2004). We have found very few research methods textbooks or dissertation guides that really explain what they mean by 'a critical approach'. One noteworthy exception to this rule is a book designed for student teachers by Poulson and Wallace (2004), whose first chapter provides a useful starting point.

Being told in feedback on your work or in coursework instructions that you have to be 'critical' is quite a challenging comment. What are you supposed to be critical about or whom are you supposed to be critical of? Are you meant to be critical of academic authors who probably know – or at least ought to know – far more about the subject than you do? If, as is the case with many Masters' students of business and management, you are new to this particular subject area, how can you have the confidence to engage 'critical debate'? And what is it anyway? Does the word have a different meaning from your previous studies in, say, education, English or engineering? And what are you supposed to do if you come from a different university cultural tradition where quoting authority figures – the 'founding fathers' of your discipline – was the norm and their wisdom was never called into question?

Critical academic inquiry can be a rather abstract concept to try to put into practice. The process of academic thinking in itself takes practice and time to develop. Most academics at least seem to agree that good critical thinking is a skill that comes through practice and that you will improve your critical reasoning skills through learning by doing. Being critical entails not only asking 'why' of the external world around you and all that you read, but also examining yourself and your own underpinning research philosophy. Thus, you need to be self-critical as well in order to demonstrate the required 'critical approach'. For example, a self-critical researcher will identify and describe their own pre-existing values that influence what they write (Bryman and Bell, 2003; Poulson and Wallace, 2004). In our case, both the authors of this text hold the view that research has a subjective quality to it and that people's values cannot be divorced from what they are researching and that this will influence how and what they write.

Although you need to show an awareness of yourself, you need also to try to maintain an open mind about other researchers' ideas until evidence indicates otherwise. This can be more difficult than it seems, especially if you have been brought up or educated with a different perspective and what you read or find out challenges your known view of the world. In addition, your scepticism or reasoned doubt about what you read and experience should be tempered by a constructive overview. Challenging the ideas and the research conducted by others is accepted practice, but you should avoid engaging in destructive criticism.

You will come across a number of traditions or strands of thinking about critical inquiry that shape much academic thinking. We will outline very briefly in the next section three of these traditions. We have described them as the paradigm debate; the analysis of argument; and learning to think critically. We think you might find these helpful in your studies of business and management literature. The labels are themselves quite contentious, but if you do get interested in this area, we have suggested some further reading at the end of the chapter. If you feel it is all beyond you, you might like to read the section below, which describes what we think is meant by 'developing a critical approach', and suggests how you can develop a critical approach in management studies. You could then skip to the critical reading section.

Approaches to Criticism in Higher Education

An ability to think, read and write critically has been considered to be an essential part of higher education for many years. In a wide-ranging review of the general aims of higher education, Ramsden (1992) found this view stated in documents over a period of

40 years in a variety of English-speaking countries including Australia, Canada, the UK and the USA and across all disciplines. Masters' programmes, at least in the UK, are designed to help you have a 'critical and informed perspective' (QAA, 2002) and key skills that you are expected to demonstrate include the ability to 'identify assumptions, evaluate statements in terms of evidence, detect false logic or reasoning, identify implicit values, define terms adequately and generalise appropriately' (QAA, 2002).

It is likely that you have had experience either within your family or a work environment of questioning a decision or the manner in which something was done. It is this 'questioning' that is the foundation of a critical approach. If you can teach yourself not to accept information at face value but to ask 'why', then you are beginning to take a critical stance and this is fundamental to your success at postgraduate level studies. This is not a wholly western academic tradition. In the Hindu educational tradition, Vedic theory encourages students to take responsibility for their own education, while the Koran encourages a questioning approach, instituted by the Prophet himself (Patel, 1994 and Phillips, 2001, cited in de Vita and Case, 2003).

The paradigm debate

One controversy surrounding approaches to research in organizational analysis and one that is worth outlining here concerns the use of single versus plural 'paradigms' in the approach to research. As a Masters' researcher, you are expected to know what a paradigm is and which one or ones you are intending to adopt for your research. It is sufficient here to say that a paradigm can be considered as an established approach to research in which academics use common theories, terminology and methods to research chosen topics. There are three key research paradigms: positivism, post-positivism and interpretivism, all of which are clearly explained in Jonathan Crix's useful book *The Foundations of Research* (2004). A 'paradigm shift' occurs when a dominant paradigm such as positivism is challenged and superseded by a different paradigm. In business and management research in Europe, a positivist approach that sought to provide an explanation for an event in an organization has been replaced (to some extent) by the use of an interpretivist approach, which tries to provide an understanding of an event.

An article by Hassard and Keleman (2002) provides an insight into this dense and confusing ongoing debate. The article covers much ground in discussing the basic principles of the different camps in approaches to organizational research. We find it helpful because so many students wish to use organizations such as multinational companies as illustrations or case studies in their dissertation and often ask for guidance on 'which paradigm to take'. Pfeffer (1993) argued that the social sciences needed to raise their credibility by pursuing a single paradigm and that by using multiple paradigms for research you end up with incomplete and vague information, which is of limited use.

The potential for vague or blurred information is also suggested by Silverman (1969) as a reason for not combining paradigms. Hassard and Kelemen (2002) respond by suggesting that a consensus will never be reached about which paradigm should be regarded as the standard, as paradigms are not static, but shift and evolve alongside the subject area. They argue that research knowledge in the social sciences, and hence in business and management, has a strongly positivist provenance because it has taken the lead from the natural science research establishment which is founded upon positivist research principles. In their view, the approaches, terminology and accepted research culture offers 'closed' meaning and prevents other interpretations that may be key to academic progress and an improved knowledge base. Authors who recommend a pragmatic approach to the choice of research paradigm include Wicks and Freeman (1998) and Weaver and Gioia (1994), who go on to suggest that a dialogue between those who champion particular research paradigms might assist in understanding and forming a balance between any inequalities and inherent weaknesses in any one approach. Organizations have changed radically over the last 20 years and so the approaches to the research of those organizations should also have developed and altered over that time to mirror those changes. Therefore these 21st-century organizations may require new and flexible research paradigms to conduct meaningful organizational research to help us better understand the business and managment environment.

Analysis of argument

Whatever you are working on, you need to be aware of how argument functions in academic study and you have to know how to respond to it. Rather than presenting evidence and then inferring from that a substantive claim to new knowledge or theory, which is how it would appear that scientists arrive at their discoveries, most people actually present arguments the other way round, by justifying claims with supporting evidence (see Chapter 10 for more on this). The process by which you justify an argument or claim involves producing reasons for why you think it is correct after you have already mentally actually arrived at that claim. The approach that natural scientists adopt, sometimes called inference, on the other hand, refers to the use of reasons to arrive at a claim. It is part of the process of analytic argumentation and the pursuit of claims that are based on universal principles.

Stephen Toulmin (1958) suggested that even in the sciences, however, justification plays an important role in argument. Although the making of discoveries is one facet of the scientist's professional work, the justification of these discoveries, by presenting supporting arguments, is another. If the function of argument is usually justification, Toulmin suggested a set of standards according to which arguments succeed or fail to stand up. An argument is judged to be sound if it is able to survive the criticisms of those who participate in the pursuit of knowledge in the same or related fields of knowledge. Of course, arguments vary from academic field to field in a variety of ways, but according to Toulmin, one of the ways that arguments do not vary is that they all may be analysed according to his layout of argument. This involves six interrelated components. The first three components, the basic elements, are described as the claim, the grounds, and the warrant. The next three components, described as the backing, the modal qualifier, and the rebuttal, modify the first three by giving the argument a context.

In Toulmin's scheme, arguments start with a claim, which is the conclusion of the argument that a person is seeking to justify. Toulmin calls the second component of an argument 'grounds'. The grounds of an argument are the facts, data or other information on which the argument is based. The third component of an argument is called the 'warrant'. The warrant assesses whether or not the journey from grounds to claim is a legitimate one. These three components are the primary elements of an argument, and in simple arguments, they may be the only components visible. Three additional elements show how practical arguments are contextualized and, thus, are different from analytic arguments, which are based on universal principles. Since the study of business is always within a context, these are crucial. The first of the three is backing in the form of context-specific data. The next element in Toulmin's layout of an argument is called a 'modal qualifier'. Modal qualifiers indicate the strength of the step that has been taken to get from the grounds to the warrant. Analytic arguments do not require modal qualifiers, because the conclusion drawn from an analytic argument is structurally certain, but justifications usually do. Some arguments include qualifiers like 'probably' or 'certainly,' indicating the confidence of the person putting forward the argument in the strength of the relationship between the data and the warrant. The final element of an argument is called the 'rebuttal', or reservation, which refers to specific circumstances when the warrant does not justify the claim. When using rebuttal, an arguer is presenting claims with a degree of caution.

Toulmin's theory of argument has had a major impact in North America, where it has become a popular tool for analysing communication and public debate, though it has had much less impact elsewhere. If you are puzzled how to analyse the argument put forward in academic writing, it may be useful to take his model and apply it to the argument in order to help you to understand its strengths and weaknesses. Numerous websites based in North American universities will help you to do this.

Learning to think critically

There is a great deal in the education literature about the role of teachers in developing students' abilities to think critically. Encouraging critical thinking is important to education in general, because of the direct link to creativity. It is the process of critical thinking applied to thought processes and ideas that enables students to come up with a creative solution. The process in education is to start with a descriptive approach, to move on to one that is critical and then from this to unlock the ability to be creative in proposing new ideas and solutions. Browne and Freeman (2000) suggest that critical thinking rests on the comprehension of the material in hand, in other words in order to be able to evaluate what you read you must be able to unearth the conclusion and the arguments that led to that conclusion. They suggest that this can be done through the use of questioning in the manner of Socrates, or just by systematically asking 'why?' They even offer a list of questions designed to aid the learner to deconstruct written material. Other writers disagree (see Bailin et al., 1999). They suggest that critical thinking is not a procedure, or a process but an iterative activity. They comment that in the education literature, critical thinking is referred to as a cognitive skill and that this equates critical thinking with mental processes and procedures, which can be improved with practice. As you read about, think and discuss your chosen management and business topic, you will become more adept at analysing the arguments and evidence put forward by others and giving your own informed opinion.

It seems that there is both a skill and an attitude aspect to critical reasoning. You need to approach the subject with a sceptical attitude, but you also have to develop the skills to utilize this scepticism in an academic context and to review constantly your own critical stance. Critical thinking within business and management can therefore be defined as the ability to reflect upon and to analyse material (such as literature) and, based on this, to make reasoned judgements. A truly critical approach will be one that is not subject specific, not process driven and incorporates practised and applied reflection.

From Criticism to Appraisal

If your first studies were in the natural sciences, you may have become familiar with debates about scientific method and the rigour of its application to solving problems that have been stated in a particular way. If you have previously studied literature, you may be used to pulling text apart or deconstructing it in order to demonstrate that you can discern meaning and engage in literary criticism. You may even have participated in a formal logic course – these are quite common in undergraduate programmes in the USA – where you have analysed the construction and use of argument or rhetoric. If you have developed skills in one or more of these areas, they may well come in useful in your business and management studies, but it is important to be aware that, as discussed in Chapter 1, studies in business and management are based around thinking and research methods derived from the social sciences. This gives a particular meaning to the idea of 'critique' or critical thinking in this subject area. The expectation at postgraduate level in business is that any person's work can be challenged, but it is the way that you challenge it that is the key.

In an interesting article that draws on a wide range of approaches to this subject, but with particular reference to the Frankfurt School of critical theory and the philosopher Habermas, Mingers (2000) suggests that there are four aspects to developing a critical approach in management education. The first is to develop critical thinking itself, which he eventually describes as the 'critique of rhetoric' (Mingers, 2000: 225). By this he means that students need to learn to appraise or evaluate a problem using a form of scepticism that is reflective – so they know why they are being critical – with an effective understanding and use of language. The other aspects he identifies are the 'critique of tradition', which is being sceptical of conventional wisdom, the 'critique of authority', which is being sceptical about one dominant view, and a 'critique of objectivity', a recognition that knowledge and information are never value-free (Mingers, 2000: 226).

It is perhaps unfortunate that we even use the word 'critical' and the verb 'to criticize' in this context. Most dictionaries define criticism as being to 'find fault with' something or some one, and critical as the process of making 'adverse judgements' or 'censorious comments'. These definitions come from the *Shorter Oxford English Dictionary* (1993). As teachers in this subject area, we are not of course really asking you to find fault with the views of the academic authors we suggest you read. We really prefer to avoid the 'c' word altogether, and to use the verb 'appraise' to describe what it is that we expect our students to be able to do when it comes to thinking and later writing about what they have read. 'Appraise' is not a word that is used very much in common English speech, but we find it useful. For a start it has a more positive sound than the 'c' word, as it contains the word 'praise' (and teachers are always being told that they do not give enough praise). Our dictionary defines 'appraise' as being to 'estimate the value or quality' of something. In our view, you therefore need to develop an approach to business and management studies whereby you try at all times to:

- **be open-minded and fair in your judgements;**

- **be sceptical about your own knowledge so that you are not over-confident in your views;**

- **ask questions constantly about the quality of your own work and any work that you are appraising;**

- **appraise arguments to see if they are convincing, once you have assessed the evidence on which they are based;**

- **be constructive – you are trying to find a better theory or result, not trying to show how clever you are by being destructively critical of someone else's work.**

Critical reading

Critical reading skills are essential to successful study in universities (Du Boulay, 1999) and beyond into your professional lives, across all management disciplines. One of the first things your teachers are likely to ask you to do is to read – they will send you a huge reading list and ask you to read for assignments from a 'wide range of sources' as discussed in Chapter 3. University teachers tend to put a lot of stress on reading articles in academic journals. Of course, academic reading itself is not assessed – only how it is used. In order to get decent marks and to learn from your reading, you need to develop the ability to read effectively, to work out the author's or authors' intentions, and to extract the essential meaning. Then all you have to do is to present your thoughts in a carefully constructed critical framework (see Chapter 7).

By the time you get to university, and even more so at postgraduate level, it is generally assumed that you already know how to read 'critically' and that you will show that you have done this in most, if not all, of your written work. But university teachers seldom tell you in so many words what they really mean by this. This leaves many students wondering how they can show in their written work that they have read something 'critically' and at what level this 'criticism' is supposed to kick in. Are you, for example, expected to be able to deliver a critique of well-known management authors such as Michael Porter? Or is it enough just to know what he has written about competitive strategy? Should you be able to describe his theories and apply them to a different context or problem? Or is it essential to find and point out any shortcomings? What happens if you can't find anything 'wrong' with it?

Becoming a critical reader does not mean that you have the ability to demonstrate that you can 'trash' papers. Finding faults, flawed argument or lack of logic in discussion or dubious methodology is only the surface level of being critical. It is not enough to flag up the shortcomings of what you have read; you also need to be able to propose alternatives. Before you start reading, you really need to consider what your prime purpose is and check whether in fact the material, texts, journal articles and other secondary data you have collected will actually fulfil your purpose. Checking this early on will save time and keep your reading focused.

Because you have so much to read and time is always tight, it is really important to read efficiently. Most academic literature is not designed to be read sequentially (as in a novel) but selectively. This is especially true of textbooks. You are expected to skim read, to skip chapters that seem to be of no use to you, to use the index to find the relevant bits, and to rely on chapter summaries and other shortcuts that occur to you to flag up the most important parts. Journal articles are usually much more condensed and written in a much less discursive way than books, but you rarely need to read every word. As you read a textbook, see if you can answer the following questions:

1 **How current is the material? Some business and management textbooks are classics, as are certain psychology texts and are valuable sources decades after publication. However, textbooks on areas such as e-commerce will date very quickly and will generally be of limited value.**

2 **What are the author's credentials? Is the author (or authors) an academic from a recognized institution or are they a business consultant? There are books published as textbooks, but which on closer inspection are really 'how to' practitioner guides with very little or no academic foundation.**

3 **How extensive is the references list at the back of the text?**

4 **Does the text reinforce ideas and concepts that you have already read about elsewhere or does it challenge those ideas?**

As a practice-based MBA or DMS student, we hope that you can see how the above applies directly to your work and management life. As a manager, you will need to be able to read documents presented to you critically and make an informed decision based on the evidence you see.

Taking notes

The way you take notes is important, as later on they will form the basis for what you write in your dissertation, and you will not have time to keep going back to the original text because something is missing. There are two issues to think about before you start to write anything down: how should you format your note-taking to be of the greatest possible use to you when you come to use them, and how to make sure you do not end up being accused of plagiarism.

If you are reading for general interest, you may like to start by asking yourself 'what, how and why' as you read (Du Boulay, 1999). You could then form straightforward categories of notes under those headings. This will give you at least three different areas to guide your comments and may help to direct your thinking. Using these three headings and the frameworks listed further on in the chapter to help you, you can create your own comments on your reading, which can now be supported by evidence. You will later need to transform your critical reading notes into an integrated critical written discussion.

If you are reading for a specific purpose, for example for an assignment or dissertation, then you can save yourself a lot of time by organizing your notes around the structure of the assignment, your main research objectives or into key themes, as you go along. For

Write up notes

Few words

Sentences

Paragraphs

Points

Figure 2.1   Building blocks

many people, this involves a completely different approach from note-taking. Many of us have got used to simply jotting down the main points from each source on a separate piece of paper and then keeping them filed by author. You need to think about how many times you will ever need to write anything that has been organized in this way? The answer is almost never. Perhaps if you were asked to do a book review it would make sense. Also if you were reading out of general interest and your notes were not related to any specific assignment, you would need to keep notes in this way. But for most purposes it makes a lot more sense to take and sort notes as you go along by theme or topic rather than by occasion or by author. If you do this rigorously, you can actually write the first draft of your literature review as you go along. You may start by noting down individual words and phrases. As you read further these isolated short notes can be built into sentences and then paragraphs as your reading and thinking develops. You should end up with a number of important points surrounded by apposite support (see Figure 2.1). (You must be scrupulous in keeping records and stating your sources.) This makes even greater sense if you are hand-writing your notes, because it is much harder to sort them into different categories later by copying and pasting them into new documents, as you could do with word-processed documents. Chapter 7 offers further guidance on different ways of categorizing and sorting information.

You do not need to keep your notes in sequential paragraphs either. Some students use learning maps to organize their note-taking, and there are computer-based tools that can help you to do this. They can be colour-coded by theme. Many students who suffer from dyslexia, which can make it much more difficult to sort and categorize notes, find it particularly helpful to use learning maps and colour codes in this way. If you see things in a visual way, this can be a very useful technique even if you are not dyslexic. In an interesting article that suggests three main ways in which she has helped postgraduate and undergraduate students at Sussex University to become better critical readers, Doreen Du Boulay suggests that students should organize their notes in tables. In the vertical column, her students put the topic and questions that they have generated and across the top, the titles of the works consulted (for example by creating a column for each work read, and giving it a key such as a, b, c, d, and so on). Full bibliographic information is kept on separate index cards. The student then looks in the various works for the answer to his or her questions or topics. The notes can then be laid out on a table as more and more columns are added, in order to make comparisons between the readings more easily. Du Boulay suggests that it also enables students to skim read more sources more quickly (Du Boulay, 1999).

When taking notes from academic journal articles or any other secondary data source, it is vital that you use your own words, or make it clear to yourself when you are not using your own words. Otherwise, when you come back to them later on, you many have forgotten which words are yours and which are copied and so are someone else's.

Make a point when taking notes of always summarizing what you read, with the original covered, so that your notes are written in your own words. You also need to take great care to acknowledge the source of the information and ideas you find and use in your work and you can help yourself to do this with careful referencing in your notes. If you do find yourself copying out great chunks of an author's work you should ask yourself why. Is it because you have not really understood what the author is saying? Read it again and then go and take a short break and do something different. When you come back to it, you may well find that your brain has started to sort out the meaning for you and that you can summarize it in your own words – but sometimes you have to give it time.

When you have taken notes about a book or an article, particularly if you have written rather a lot, it can be really helpful later on if you write a very brief summary at the end. This summary should be only a couple of sentences and should record your instant reaction. It should say how what you thought about the key message or messages you identified in your reading. When you come back to it – often many months later – you might not agree with your instant reaction, but it will give you a vivid picture of how you actually felt about what you read at the time and you may be able to incorporate it into your literature review.

Using quotations

It is also a good idea to think about what you need to record. When you take notes, the temptation is to write too much down because you do not want to go back to the original when you are writing up. Many students think it is useful to use a lot of quotations, for example, so they copy out chunks of text into their notes. They think it makes their work look erudite. This is not, however, how it appears to the teachers who mark it. As a general rule, it is much better to avoid using quotations in your written work unless the words are really worth quoting. You are not writing an essay on English literature; you have probably been asked to write some sort of business report or a dissertation. Most quotations from textbooks and leading authors are not really worth quoting. A business assignment that is peppered with quotations can look disjointed and as if you have not fully understood what you are writing about. If you really must use a quotation, it should be brief. If you still think that someone is worth quoting, you do need to *copy the words and the punctuation exactly in your notes,* 'put quotation marks round the words you are quoting', and record precisely where it came from, *including* the full bibliographic reference and the page number, (or full web page address and the date you accessed it).

Plagiarism

You must take great care when taking notes that you do not leave yourself open to accusations of plagiarism later on. Plagiarism – using the work of others without making it clear that you have done so – includes using words more or less exactly as they are found in articles, books, newspapers or any other secondary source, including the Internet; using other people's ideas without acknowledging them; and paraphrasing what you read or hear without saying where it came from. 'Patching' is a form of plagiarism that occurs when you take a central phrase or idea from an author without acknowledging it and then write your own words around that idea, to form a paragraph or section of your written work. An example of patching would be using the phrase *game theory has revolutionized ways of thinking about social problems in general and business in particular,* and going on to construct a paragraph about the role of game theory in thinking about business strategy. The reason that this is patching is that the words we have put in italics were taken from Igor Ansoff's book on corporate strategy, entitled *Corporate Strategy.* In order to use the words you would have to acknowledge the source in a reference, put the words in quotation marks and give the original page number, which was page 105 in the Pelican edition of 1973. It is also plagiarism to take a concept such as the 'value chain' to discuss efficiencies in the operations of a company, without citing the author, in this case Michael Porter. At Masters' level, it is advisable to return to the original source and to read it, rather than a later reference to it. In this case, you would read M.E. Porter (1980), *Competitive Advantage,* published by The Free Press, New York and reference this in your work.

It is unfortunately quite easy to plagiarize without really intending to do so. Many universities now use electronic search software to find phrases and whole paragraphs that have been lifted from academic sources and incorporated into student assignments. Most students do not necessarily mean to plagiarize, but time pressures, being unsure of how to communicate complex ideas in an appropriate academic language and also coming from an educational background where reiterating published authors' words is considered good practice makes plagiarism more likely.

Whether it was deliberate or unintentional, universities take plagiarism very seriously. The penalties for being caught usually start with an automatic zero for the piece of work found to have been plagiarized and can result in failing your Masters' degree. Plagiarism is a serious issue because it is dishonest and devalues the hard work of academics who have produced the original work. It is also counter to the underpinning foundation of academic endeavour at universities in searching for contributions to knowledge. If universities did not penalize those students who plagiarize, the currency of the degrees offered would be completely undermined. Increasingly, plagiarism is seen as unethical and immoral behaviour and universities are now under pressure to search out and actively deal with those who plagiarize. Finally, committing plagiarism is completely unfair to those students who write using their own words and ideas.

Summary

In this chapter we have looked at why, in order to satisfy the academic requirements of a Masters' degree, you have to develop a critical approach to the subject and how you can go about it. We have offered advice on how to develop your critical reading skills, how take notes and use quotations, and how to avoid plagiarism.

Discussion Questions

1   To what extent is it possible to be positive when using a critical approach?

2   What does a critical approach entail?

Further Reading

Poulson, L. and Wallace, M. (eds) (2004) *Learning to Read Critically in Teaching and Learning.* London: Sage. Although this particular book is not designed for business students, the first chapter provides a valuable base for developing a critical approach.

3 Generating, Developing and Mapping Ideas for Research Topics

What Am I Going to Write About?

Many students have difficulty in thinking of and then formulating a topic that is suitable for a dissertation. In particular, students seem to have two main problems. Some have difficulties with coming up with any sort of topic in the first place. Others find this no problem, but then struggle both to format and arrange their ideas and to build on the links between them. Both groups can have problems with relating ideas to topics that are 'suitable' and fall within academic and course boundaries. Scaling up topics that seem too small and containing those that are too big are also common problems. The first part of this chapter helps you to come up with some ideas that make good dissertation topics. The second part shows how you can create a visual pattern of ideas through drawing learning maps or spider diagrams and using decision trees to show the progression of thought and possible dead ends. It also looks at how to scope and focus topics so that they are realistic and achievable.

Techniques and Tools for Finding a Topic

Finding a suitable initial topic to develop into a feasible dissertation that is researchable can seem a difficult task. This is a particular problem for students who have started on a Masters' programme and who have neither studied the subject before nor had much work experience. However, there are lots of techniques that can help you if you are feeling lost. MBA and DMS students may have much less difficulty in finding a topic because it is almost bound to be related either to current work or to a project or business idea that has arisen from work experiences. Formatting your ideas and relating them to suitable core academic topics may be more of a problem.

Brainstorming with your friends

It can be very helpful to brainstorm ideas for dissertations with a group of friends, perhaps a group of people from the same course who are all facing similar difficulties in finding a topic and are prepared to share any preliminary thoughts and ideas. It is useful to follow the 'rules' of brainstorming, which are very simple. The aim is to break through the barriers we all put up in our minds to enable the participants to be flexible and creative. This facilitates original thinking. A cardinal rule is to allow no criticism of other people's ideas, or of your own, while the brainstorm is in progress, and to write every suggestion, no matter how seemingly silly, down. So, for your brainstorming session you will need a large space, preferably one where you can write things down on paper and later stick it up on the walls (a classroom is ideal), and someone who is prepared to write down the ideas. There is no limit on the number of people who can participate, but you do need more than two. Some textbooks suggest brainstorming on your own, but in practice this is quite difficult to achieve without the external stimulus of other people's suggestions triggering your own thoughts. When you have written down and displayed all the different ideas, you can then start to make some judgements about them. Find the most outlandish and see if you can turn it round collectively so that it could make a good dissertation topic, and then the next most outlandish, and so on. Write these refined topics on a separate sheet and discard the rest. Return to your brainstorm and repeat the process until you have a reasonable number – it is up to you to judge how many – of topics that have passed the first test. Use the checklist later in this chapter to help you evaluate their suitability.

Even after going through this process you may find that you are still not particularly happy with any of the topics on your lists. Do not despair; the brainstorming process may have sufficiently loosened your thinking process that you will later find it relatively simple to come up with a topic on your own.

Browsing the library shelves

One very simple way of finding ideas is to browse the library shelves and to search electronic library catalogues to determine what is being written about in the business and management subject area. This may give you ideas about current popular themes and who are the major authors. You could leaf through some of these books and look at the main themes they deal with simply by looking at chapter headings in the contents pages.

Building on a piece of course work

Other courses you have studied and texts you have read for your Masters' course may produce references worth following up and could lead to you identifying a specific research topic. For example, we have found that courses on consumer behaviour or international management frequently result in Masters' students' dissertation topics in those areas. You may like to develop further a piece of work you have done as an assignment on a topic that has fascinated you. A particularly good piece of work, or one where you have felt that you were only covering just the surface of the subject and would like to go into it in much greater depth may make a suitable starting point for a dissertation. You must be careful to make sure that there really is a much greater depth that you can get into, because writing a dissertation is a much more disciplined and lengthy task than writing an assignment. Also if the original assignment was a piece of group work you must deal with the fact that it was not all your own work.

Finding a topic by using a textbook

If you are starting from scratch, one approach is to think about what are the five areas of management that you are likely to cover in your course? If it is a DMS or MBA they are likely to be:

- **marketing;**

- **human resources;**

- **accounting and finance;**

- **organizational behaviour;**

- **strategy.**

If it is another Masters' course, you can look in your course guide for a list of the main modules or components of your programme. Look at the list and take any one of these large topic areas and find just one mainstream textbook that deals with the subject; for example, for marketing it might be Brassington and Pettitt (2003) *Principles of Marketing*, or for organizational behaviour it might be Mullins (1999), *Management and Organizational Behaviour*, for strategy it might be Johnson et al. (2005) *Exploring Corporate Strategy*, or for human resource management it might be Armstrong (2003) *A Handbook of Human Resource Management Practice*. Your course guide will probably list more than one such textbook for each area.

Look in the book at the main chapter headings and select a chapter that takes your fancy or – if you are truly desperate – one at random, ignoring the first and the last chapters, which are likely to be an introduction and a concluding chapter. Look at one chapter and write down the main subheadings, as if each were a possible dissertation topic. Next check each possible heading against the course requirements for your programme. Some will not comply. How would you amend them so that they would comply with the requirements? Knock out those that are obviously unsuitable. Assuming you now have six or eight, they will still be fairly general – too general to make a good dissertation. Start to think about how you could relate them to something that is researchable within the boundaries you have got, which includes time, distance, money and access or lack of it to organizations. Can you confine it within one particular country, sector, business type or organization? Can you relate it to something you already know a little bit about? Does it interest you sufficiently to develop into a dissertation research proposal? If you cannot give a definite 'yes' to these questions, go back and try another topic area and textbook.

Using your paid or voluntary work as a source of dissertation topics

A past role at work or an experience at work such as an appraisal or being part of a project team could form the core topic for your dissertation or project. If you are working either full- or part-time, you may have ideas for topics based on your work. Try jotting down a list of the day's activities. Were there events in that day that could relate to academic literature on business and management that you could develop into a topic for your dissertation? Be creative!

There may be issues or problems that your organization is currently trying to solve or issues you have identified that are particularly relevant to the business sector you are working in. For example, your aim may be to try to explain why the market share is falling for a product your company produces, or whether key account management is proving effective for the sales department. In some cases, your line manager may even suggest you investigate a particular topic, but this will need to meet the approval of the university or college where you are studying as well.

Even a part-time job that seems not to have any management content or to deal directly with concepts you have read about in the business and management literature can have potential. Meeting and talking to customers or clients in your capacity as a bartender or shop assistant may create research opportunities; for example, a wrong order may lead to the need to correct the mistake and thus service recovery becomes a topic you could investigate further. Working in service industries, even in a junior role, can bring you into contact with managers and if you get the opportunity it may be worth discussing your ideas and aspirations with them.

If you are involved in voluntary or community work, that too can be a fertile source of topics for research. We have had students who have been heavily involved with charitable fundraising, the organization of meals on wheels services for the elderly, or who have a family involvement with charitable or religious organizations, who have found good dissertation topics in these areas. These types of organizations may welcome your attention and be anxious to learn what a fresh pair of eyes makes of what they do.

Asking friends and family

You could ask friends and family for suggestions for topics that stem from their own working experience. In the past, fathers were useful sources of suggestions for students, but mothers increasingly now have business roles and can be quizzed for ideas. However, you may not be as enthusiastic or as motivated when it comes to doing research into someone else's idea rather than your own. You also need to check these ideas carefully against the course requirements and for their feasibility. It is better not to get pushed into trying to do something to 'help' the family business if it really does not match the course requirements or your personal research interests. On the other hand, you should have little problem getting access to primary data, and that can be a key consideration.

Your career goals

The aspirations you have about work and the type of career you wish to pursue can also guide your choice of research topics. Masters' students frequently choose topics that they wish to know more about in order to start or progress in that area for their career. For example, one of our students used a dissertation investigating the successful promotional campaigns surrounding the market entry of premium pre-mixed drinks as a vehicle to get an interview with an advertising agency, and as a result was offered a management job. Be realistic about this, though. Just because you have written a good dissertation on business ethics in the oil industry does not mean that you will land a job with an oil company, though a good mark in your dissertation may well enhance the look of your curriculum vitae (resumé).

Building on other activities

Another way of finding a topic for a dissertation is to build on something you do already and enjoy. This can be particularly useful if you are involved in activities that take up a great deal of time and about which you have specialist knowledge, and good contacts, such as the arts, or sports such as rowing and rugby. These contacts could prove useful for helping to gain access when you are undertaking primary research and should not be underestimated. For example, several of our students participate in sports and we have recently successfully supervised dissertations on the marketing of county cricket, on the use of sponsorship in rugby football and on the business strategies pursued by small companies producing equipment for championship rowers. In all cases, the students were able to use the fact that they had very good contacts as a result of spending long hours in training, and were able to use some of the time they had to spend hanging around at regattas and sports grounds to collect primary data from interviews with suppliers, customers, sponsors and administrators within their sports. Another student used her experience as an amateur actor to write a dissertation about the marketing of open-air theatre productions.

As a consumer of products, take a walk around your local town shopping area. What events, images and activities do you notice? How do these relate to what you know about marketing, retailing or buyer behaviour? Which of these could be developed into a research topic?

Looking at past theses and dissertations

Another useful technique for finding a topic is to look at past dissertations, either at undergraduate or Masters' level. Most institutions keep lists of past titles or at least abstracts, or even full versions of the better ones for you to read in the library or research centre. You will be able to tell from the lists what have been the most popular topic areas and this may influence you towards or away from them.

Looking at current management issues

The business press may be a source of inspiration for you for topic ideas, but you do need to be sure that today's topic is not so new that there is no coherent management literature that it could be easily related to. Read a couple of recent copies of the *Economist* or the *McKinsey Quarterly Review* and write down the current management issues you find discussed or dealt with there. When you have done this, go through your list, prioritizing issues that most appeal to you. Can you work one or two of them up into a suitable topic for a dissertation?

Journal articles as a source of research topics

It is worth searching online academic journal databases to find out what management topics academics are currently writing about. You can search under key words or just browse journals issue by issue. Recent popular research topics in business and management include the Internet and virtual marketplace, change management, the globalization of business, corporate social responsibility, brand management, mergers and acquisitions activity, foreign direct investment strategies and the growth of small businesses.

Reading journal articles that are literature reviews on specific themes, and that chart the progression of research in a certain area, can act as a useful starting block. These articles outline what research has already been done in a particular field and may give you several ideas or suggest the possibility of extending a past piece of research. It is particularly helpful to find those articles that suggest that the authors have piloted a method or started a piece of research in one particular area but where 'more needs to be done', as these can really get you started and provide a platform from which you can extend the reading by augmenting the literature review and the primary research by reproducing it in another area or under different conditions. If you are very lucky, a quick email to the authors of the article saying that you are considering doing this may elicit a very positive and friendly response.

You may also use an article as a point of comparison for your own research. You could take something that has been researched before, and simply replicate it, but to a different sample or in a different country. You could then compare the results with the original findings. This is perfectly acceptable, as long as you can justify the approach in your dissertation. It can be done across companies, sectors, countries and products. For example, one of our students replicated a study about online shopping behaviour among students in her research. She then compared her results with a recently published American study in her dissertation and she came up with some real insight into the differences in behaviour.

Another way to find a topic from looking through academic journals is to think about the more abstract concepts such as trust, risk, relationships, loyalty, motivation, and so on, that lie behind some of these articles. You could then explore what the business literature says about these concepts and perhaps apply them to a specific sector or company. Conceptual journal articles that discuss ideas and concepts could also be exploited as a jumping off point, as the ideas could be taken and tested out by you in a practical context. For example, you could extend an article that describes the theoretical aspects of loyalty by choosing to try to identify the aspects of loyalty that a certain group of employees held, or a group of supermarket shoppers.

The debate and disagreement between authors in published articles may also provide ideas for topics. Contradictory views can stimulate your own ideas and creativity. For example, there has been a series of articles in the journal *Human Relations* where Gert Hofstede's theories about national cultural characteristics have been attacked and defended (McSweeney, 2002a, 2002b; Hofstede, 2002).

Journal articles can also provide a framework or model that you may wish to apply to a different context. A good topic for a Masters' dissertation is to take a theory that you have read about from one area and to test it out in a totally different one to see if it is still applicable. For example, the brands box model (de Chernatony and

McWilliam, 1989) was originally developed as a theory to help managers to better understand the nature of their brands, and was then tested in the context of well-known brands of physical consumer goods (de Chernatony and McWilliam, 1990). A colleague of ours took the idea, replicated the research design, and applied it to the branding of destinations in the tourism sector, finding that generally it fitted quite well (Clarke, 2000).

Relating your ideas to suitable core academic topics

Many MBA and DMS students arrive at college or university with a burning interest in a particular topic, but find it quite a struggle to turn it into a viable dissertation topic that satisfies academic requirements. Your topic might well be of interest to you because it relates to a current or recent issue at work, such as how to market green energy, how to sort out succession planning in a family-owned business, or how to increase the motivation of healthcare workers in lower administrative grades. It can be very difficult to see the link between these practical issues and a core academic topic, or a coherent body of academic management literature, or 'literature stream'. Clearly, in the examples quoted above the first is obviously about marketing and the second and third are to do with human relations. But these subject areas are far too vast to be described as a coherent management literature. The topic needs to be scoped or narrowed down before it can become a feasible topic for a dissertation (see below for how to do this).

Checklist: What Makes a Good Research Topic?

As you search around and come up with ideas for your research you need to filter all your ideas to find one or two feasible topics. Here is a list of questions that will assist in the filtering process. You may need to add to them or modify them, depending on the specific requirements of your course.

✓ Does it fit the specifications and meet the standards of the course I am doing?
✓ Does it contain a central business or management issue?
✓ Does it have some underpinning theory? (See Chapter 1)
✓ Will it provide new insights into some aspect of business and management?
✓ Is it an area that I am really interested in?

✓ Is it researchable by using primary or secondary data that I can collect myself?
✓ Have I got or can I develop the research skills needed to complete it?
✓ Does it match my career goals?
✓ Can I do it within the time and any finance constraints?

If your topic does not meet the specifications set by your course, you must reject it straightaway and find one that does. For example, if your dissertation is required to be in the area of 'international management' and is only about national managers in one country, it is likely to be rejected as a topic because it does not match the specification. You can either then try to make it international or choose something that does fit the rules.

Practical Worked Examples

Using a Textbook to Find a Dissertation Topic

One of the main textbooks that many courses use for human resource management is a huge book by Michael Armstrong (Armstrong, 2003). If you knew you wanted to write a dissertation in this subject area, but were stuck for a topic, looking through the contents pages, which list 12 parts to the book and 59 chapters, could give you a start. Not all the chapter headings would make a suitable topic for a dissertation, but you could begin by looking more closely at the chapters on performance management, learning, job evaluation, the characteristics of people at work, motivation, job satisfaction, reward and organizational culture.

How James Smith Came Up with an Idea for his Dissertation

James knew he had to write a dissertation and that he had to find a suitable idea that could be developed into a 'proper' topic with research aims and questions, and that he could research and write up in the next 9 months. But where could he start? Every idea he had seemed too big or too vague. Could he research something on Foreign Direct Investment (FDI)? His tutors told him this was too wide an area and he must narrow it down, but how was he going to do this when he knew little about the subject anyway? He was really interested in FDI and couldn't face spending so long writing a dissertation that didn't interest him. Perhaps there was a way of linking FDI with his holiday work experience in an engineering company? The company made braking systems that were sold to several major car manufacturers with production plants on several continents.

James drew up a list of possible connected questions by jotting them down over the next few days:

- How did those car manufacturers decide which country markets to enter?
- Why did those companies choose his firm to buy braking systems from as opposed to other firms?
- Did car manufacturers prefer overseas manufacture rather than direct import and, if so, why?
- What were the relationships between parts suppliers, such as his firm, and the car manufacturers based on?
- Why weren't local firms chosen to make the braking systems?
- What were the long-term implications for the manufacturers using 'external' suppliers?
- Was it worthwhile forming alliances with host country manufacturers as part of the longer-term strategy?

When he read through his list of questions, James realized that he had the basis of an idea. The research area could be identified as suppliers, manufacturers, FDI and the relationships between them! His chosen sector was going to be the car manufacturing industry, but now he knew what his all-important academic themes were going to be. James decided to spend his next free day in the library exploring what was available on the themes of supplier, manufacturer relationships and decisions about foreign direct investments. A search in the catalogue showed 44 books, including those with authors such as the European Union (EU), International Monetary Fund (IMF), Organisation for Economic Cooperation and Development (OECD) and United Nations Conference on Trade and Development (UNCTAD); several hundred journal articles on the electronic journal databases; and sixteen past Master's dissertations. There was obviously a lot of reading to do, but an email from his tutor reassured him that he was on the right path. Now all he had to do was find the time to read and to scope his project to make it realistic and achievable in the next nine months!

Developing and Mapping Ideas

Once you have an idea, or several ideas, for your dissertation, you need to develop your topic. For all Masters' students, whether studying for an MA, MSc or MBA/DMS, the conceptual focus and scope needs clarification and for MBA and DMS students in particular, the initial ideas need to be checked to see if they are viable for the organization concerned. You need to 'scope' your topic. One way of helping yourself to clearly develop and expand your initial idea, and to find out where the boundaries are, is to draw a learning map.

Learning maps are also known as mind maps (Buzan, 1988 [1977]) or spider diagrams. They are a useful tool to help you plot and visualize your ideas, and to enable you to see the scale and scope of the task you have taken on. They consist of individual diagrams containing a central theme or concept around which other related themes or concepts are plotted. These diagrams consist of a clearly defined central idea with key words and associations fanning out from the central point. A clustering of associated themes may occur and you can use colour coding to identify particularly interesting topics or to denote relative importance. James Smith, in the example above, could have drawn a learning map with the central theme of FDI, and separate clusters for suppliers and manufacturers from which he could develop any associations or related aspects as they came to him, before, during or after his reading on the subjects. Later, he might choose a different colour for each of the three central aspects.

This pictorial method of thought mapping has received wide acclaim for its simplicity of approach. The creation of learning maps incorporates whole brain thinking rather than left-or right-side dominance, balancing the logic of the left hemisphere with the creativity of the right hemisphere (Buzan, 1988 [1977]; De Bono 1977). Since the way we think is not always logical or rational, when ideas come to us they are rarely in order. People do not necessarily process information starting with A and working through the alphabet to Z; instead they are far more likely to start with S, move to E followed by Q and end with A. Learning maps take account of this, as the structure allows the addition of new information and makes explicit how one area connects to another.

We use learning maps with our students to encourage them to be creative in how they might approach their research and in their subsequent strategies for the research. The three main types of creativity (creation, synthesis and modification) can be captured in a learning map. Creation occurs from the initial drawing of a map of your ideas of a topic or a series of topics. The synthesis takes place as you identify connections and various linkages that are present when you look at the map. You may decide that certain connections are worth further investigation. Then as you expand and develop your learning map, you will make changes and alterations and thus engage in the process of modification.

Learning maps can also act as a catalyst in creative problem-solving, as they often give visual clues and links that otherwise you might overlook. Because when you draw a learning map you form loosely associated pathways of research topics and ideas, your diagram can make new possibilities explicit. You would probably not have noticed the linkages if you had written an ordinary list. Problems that can be solved in a creative way vary widely in their complexity, as do the maps made to resolve them. You can also make learning maps in groups, with friends and other students – the encouragement, active help and co-participation of the group members can enhance the output from the creative problem-solving. There is no judgement as to what is 'right' or 'wrong' on a learning map, but any subsequent discussion may outline the most feasible or preferred option.

Once you have drawn one or several learning maps, you will need to return to the requirements of your course and institution to ensure that you are developing relevant ideas. It is quite common to end up with several learning maps, parts of which are fascinating but may not be appropriate for your research requirements. As you get further into your stride, you may find yourself thinking again about your purpose in pursuing research on this topic. You also need to check again if the aims are realistic and achievable. You can try some feasibility checks on your ideas and on the limit of the boundaries (how far you are going to go) as you go along. Use the topic checklist suggested above, or ask yourself again if you can answer, honestly, the following questions:

- **Is this really of contemporary management significance?**

- **Am I sure that I can gather empirical data to investigate it?**

- **Is there theory available to underpin my discussion?**

- **Am I certain that it meets the criteria set out by my course and institution?**

Alternatively, you could compile a straightforward list of strengths and weaknesses of your topic, and check carefully that you can remedy or minimize the impact of any weaknesses. You could ask a fellow student to do it for you in return for checking through his or her topic. One diagnostic tool you may wish to employ to assess your topic's feasibility is force field analysis. To create a force field analysis, place the topic in the middle of a piece of paper and on one side write a list of reasons for not doing the topic and on the other side a number of reasons in favour of doing the topic (see Figure 3.1). This gives an overview of the topic. You can even weight certain factors with different scores (5 could be the most important factor with 1 being the least important), which you think are especially important. You can then add up each side

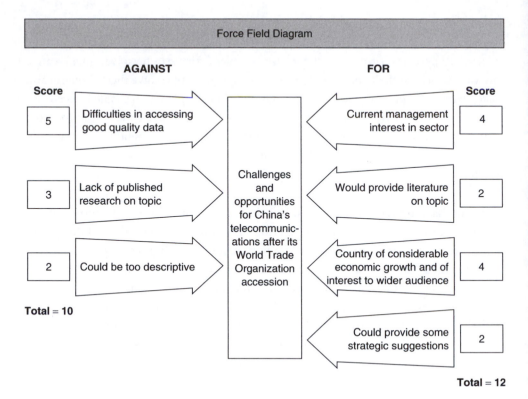

	AGAINST		FOR	
Score				**Score**
5	Difficulties in accessing good quality data		Current management interest in sector	4
3	Lack of published research on topic	Challenges and opportunities for China's telecommunic-ations after its World Trade Organization accession	Would provide literature on topic	2
2	Could be too descriptive		Country of considerable economic growth and of interest to wider audience	4
			Could provide some strategic suggestions	2

Force Field Diagram

Total = 10

Total = 12

Figure 3.1   Force field diagram

and total the scores. The side with the highest total, either for or against your topic, is then clear.

Practical Worked Example

How to Learn How to Draw Learning Maps

It is often easier to practise a new technique such as drawing learning maps on a subject you already know something about. Figure 3.2 gives an example of a learning map on the topic of English food created by a group of international MSc students studying International Management.

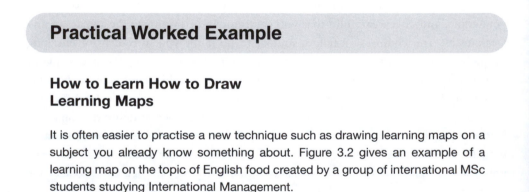

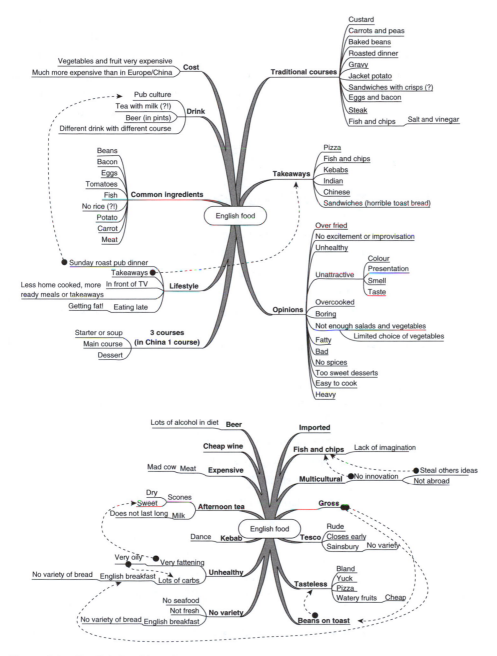

Figure 3.2   English food learning maps

Summary

This chapter has suggested various techniques to help you to identify research topics for a dissertation. Academic approaches through exploring academic literature and experience-based searches are equally valid ways to identify a suitable topic. Visual tools such as learning maps can be useful in helping you to identify and plan out ideas for your research. Checking on the suitability of your ideas and your learning maps for your dissertation can be done by either conducting an evaluation of their strengths and weaknesses or by using techniques such as force field analysis. They must always be cross-checked for their suitability as against the requirements of your course.

Suggested Activity

Deciding on a Topic for a Dissertation

1 Choose four possible projects that you like.
2 For each one write down the answer to these questions:
   a Why does this project appeal to me?
   b What is good about it?
3 Give each one a score out of 5 for appeal and out of 5 for attributes that you think are good. Add up the total.
4 Take the project with the highest score and write down the answer to these questions:
   a What research questions are suggested by the research topic?
   b To what area of business and management academic literature does your research topic relate?
5 Consider: do you want to do primary research?
   a How will you get access to your research subjects?
   b What are the practical obstacles?
6 Is it still looking good? No? Go back two steps and start with the topic with the next highest score

Suggested Activity

Developing and Mapping your Ideas

Once you have created a list of vague questions such as James Smith did or have a couple of research topic areas you have found from textbooks that you would ike to explore further, draw a learning map for each of these. You can use a separate sheet of paper for each and see how far you can get with each idea. You may reach

(Continued)

(Continued)

a dead end; if so, go on to the next idea or question and then return to the others later on. Don't worry if it appears messy or illogical; just keep going until you have put down all the possible associations you can come up with. Mapping out your ideas will help you to progress your thoughts about the subject. Drawing and mapping may take more than a day to do, but by the end you should be able to identify which map and even which part of which map you wish to pursue further. It is worth keeping these maps for reference later. You can also try showing them to your tutor or supervisor for further ideas and discussion.

Discussion Questions

1 Why is it important to screen your dissertation ideas at an early stage?

2 What constitutes a 'good' research project?

3 What advantages might there be in creating a 'learning map' of your ideas?

Further Reading

Buzan, Tony (2003) *The Mind Map Book* **(revised edition). London: BBC**; and **Buzan, Tony (1988) [1977]** *Make the Most of Your Mind.* **London: Pan.** How to improve your memory, take notes, enhance your creativity, and improve your ability to make judgements.

Svantesson, I. (1998) *Learning Maps and Memory Skills* **(2nd edition). London: Kogan Page.** A simple guide to how to get started on learning maps and how to use them to organize your thinking.

4 Making your Project Manageable
How Far Should I Go?

As a researcher, you will find that you need to establish boundaries to your research, so that you know how much you need to do. This chapter helps you to make decisions about these boundaries, so you can make sure that your project is manageable. It also helps you to assess the feasibility of your project given your resource constraints. If you are an MBA or DMS student, the sorts of boundaries we are talking about will also include issues such as the politics of the organization where you hope to carry out your research, which may set its own limits on the extent of your research, and your own career goals. If you are an MA or MSc student, the boundaries to what you can do are likely to be more to do with the availability of information and access to an organization to collect data. In this chapter, we help you to turn your research topic ideas into achievable research objectives, questions and hypotheses that you can act on.

Establishing Boundaries

Once you have reached a decision on your research topic area (see Chapter 3), you need to return to earth and run a rigorous reality check over it. Use the checklist in Chapter 3 to make sure that your topic really will fit with what your institution requires and what you will be able to achieve in the time allowed. If you are dependent on help from an organization, now is the time to start negotiating with the people who can give you access and help with the progress of your project (for more on this, see the section on access later in the chapter).

One of the first decisions you have to make is how far you can go with your research – you need to establish parameters and boundaries for your research. Use your learning map to help you to decide, perhaps in discussion with your tutors, which areas you are going to include and which to exclude at the beginning. You could choose to include your learning map as an appendix in your dissertation to demonstrate to an examiner your understanding of how interconnected certain themes and topics are within management research, but to show that you have decided to focus on only one or two of those themes. You will have demonstrated your knowledge about the extent of the subject by doing this and also will have shown that you are capable of focus.

There is often a temptation to try and include too much in a dissertation at too super-ficial a level. At postgraduate level, a dissertation should show depth of knowledge about a narrow specified subject area. You are aiming to write a lot about a little and not the other way round. Masters' students can get upset by this, as it appears that the dis-sertation is limiting their potential to show everything they know about a subject. Many initial topics and proposals are far too broad to be achievable. Recently, we turned one down that was on the role of women in the economic development of Asia. It is a fas-cinating topic and the student had struggled valiantly to try and confine it within the scope of a Masters' dissertation, but the topic was just too big and not really reducible to a small-scale piece of work. In the end, she chose a completely different topic for her dissertation.

As your research progresses, it can be helpful to draw further more detailed learning maps of the themes in your reading as your knowledge of the subject develops. You can then highlight themes you are continuing to pursue and the extent of your progress. This could form useful material for your reflective journal, if you need to write one, or for the overview part of your eventual literature review (see Figure 4.1).

Positioning your Research

In some universities, particularly continental European ones, there exists a specific requirement to discuss the 'positioning' of your proposed research in the research pro-posal, and, indeed, in the finished dissertation. It is important to understand what 'the positioning of your research' means. A positioning statement should outline how your research project fits into what has already been written in that topic area. Until you have done a certain amount of surface reading, your first initial sweep of the relevant literature, you will not be able to position your research. You therefore need to start reading at an early stage. Your initial reading may show that very little research has been done in your precise topic area and that your project could assist in 'plugging the research gap'. Your reading might perhaps direct you to one model that you could apply to a different industry sector. Once you have had your initial idea, extended and devel-oped it using learning maps (see Chapter 3), and identified the main key authors that you will be reading thoroughly, you will be able to position your research. You can incorporate an outline of the limitations of previous research and how your proposed research will not repeat these limitations in your discussion. Some students find it help-ful to construct a Venn diagram of the overlaps, intersections and gaps identified in the published literature that shows where their research will be positioned.

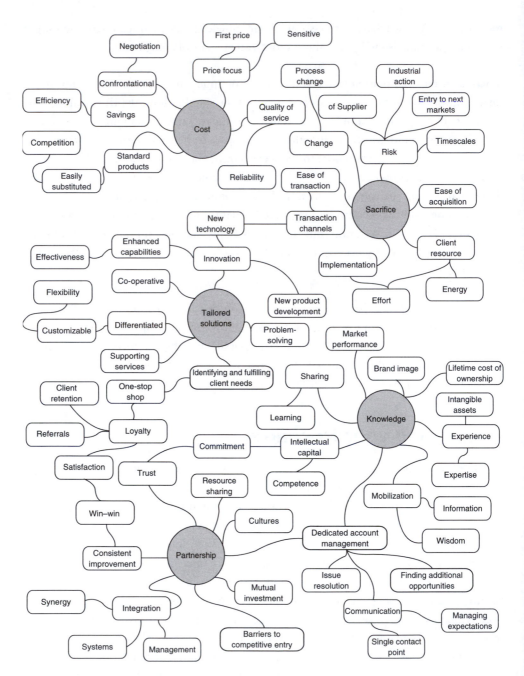

Figure 4.1   Brainstorm on value

When you make your positioning statement, it should include an assessment of the value that you think that it will add to the existing body of knowledge on that subject. You may wish to describe what your expected outcome is likely to be – an amended theory, a new framework to be tested in future research, specific sector findings that will be of use to practitioners, and so on. Your positioning statement should indicate why the dissertation would be worth reading and where the boundaries of the research project lie. It is worth being explicit about boundaries; that is, what you are not going to cover that may be relevant or linked to your research topic, and why you have chosen not to include some areas. This discussion does not need to be lengthy, but should go beyond what we as examiners frequently read, for example, 'topic z will not be included in the dissertation because it is outside the parameters of the research', to which our response is 'please explain why'.

Developing your Topic into Research Objectives, Questions and/or Hypotheses

Once you have established some rough boundaries to your research, you should be ready to do some more work to pinpoint your precise research questions and to link them to objectives. In the books on research methods, there is quite a lot of discussion about the use of hypotheses, objectives and research questions, and different authors use different terminology for what is essentially the same thing. This can be very confusing. What is undoubtedly the case is that before you plunge into your research, you need to have a very clear idea of what you expect the outcomes to be and that you will be asked to express your precise aims and objectives, both in your dissertation and your research proposal (see below).

Some books suggest that you express your aims as a research problem or problems (Thietart et al., 2001) as opposed to a research question or questions (Punch, 2000), but they amount to the same thing – a clear idea of what you are trying to do in your dissertation. A 'research problem' may conjure up a slightly negative image in your mind and an objective could be something that you may not actually get to, while a question requires an answer but has a more neutral tone. Another way of thinking about it is to see your dissertation as a research puzzle, so you could ask yourself 'What puzzle am I trying to solve by doing my research?' or even 'What exactly am I trying to find out?' Whether you are writing research objectives to put in your proposal or research questions, it is helpful to start from a central research question, which is also sometimes referred to as the central management issue, which is basically what you are trying to find out. It may form part or all of your title.

Writing Research Objectives or Questions

Some institutions demand that you write a list of your research questions, others that you list your research objectives. You should follow the convention adopted by your course, if there is one. Either way, being able to express exactly what it is that you want to find out is crucial to the success of your project. Clear research questions or objectives enable you to check regularly whether the research and reading you are doing actually answers the questions or meets the objectives. Your institution may advise you on the preferred number of objectives or research questions. Generally, more than one and fewer than six is acceptable. The nature of the objectives and questions should reflect the type of contribution that will be made by the research. Will the outcome be largely theoretical? This may be quite likely in an MA or MSc dissertation. Or will the results have a practical management application? This is more likely in an MBA/DMS dissertation.

In business research, particularly for an MBA or DMS project, your work may be about a particular problem in an organization that requires a solution. In practice, you may find that there will be little choice over what will form the central management issue or the main objectives of your research. In some consultancy projects, you may be asked to intervene to put your proposed solution into practice and your dissertation may include a reflection on the process and how it worked. It is sometimes not possible to know at the beginning of a project of this type what all your research questions are going to be, as the process of implementation will throw up new ones. Whatever you find out during the course of your research should help to explain or add understanding to the reality of management.

Research Questions

Writing about social research, and with a lot of experience in research into teaching, Punch (2000) suggests that you can look at the development of research questions as a hierarchy, with the areas becoming narrower and more specific as you work downwards. You start by defining your research area and you then narrow it down to one topic. From this you can then develop general research questions, which can be further divided into specific research questions. At a later stage, you will also have data collection questions such as those you might use in a questionnaire (Punch, 2000).

When people write research questions, they tend initially to start with 'What?' but you also really need to ask some 'why' and 'how' questions as your research develops. Your final list of research questions must be capable of being answered or met by your research within the time and resources that you have available. You therefore need to ask relevant questions that are phrased correctly, so that you can collect data that will produce meaningful conclusions.

You might like to consider applying the following generic research questions to your topic:

1 **What is X like?**

A question of description, 'What is x like' can be expressed as 'What are the elements of trust online?'

2 **Is X different from Y?**

A question of comparison could be expressed as: 'Do expatriate managers structure their teams differently from native managers in international firms?'

3 **Does X cause Y?**

A question of causality could be expressed as: 'Does increased investment in human resource policies benefit company performance?'

4 **Does X cause more change in Y than Z?**

A causality and comparative question could be expressed as: 'Does the introduction of performance related pay increase manager productivity more than better training?'

Research Objectives

Your research objectives will draw together the various strands and variables of the project and need to be written clearly and concisely. These objectives may stand on their own, or alternatively you can develop specific research questions which, when answered, will enable you to achieve your objectives.

Typical research objectives for a dissertation in international business might include:

- one that relates to the business sector or industry in the relevant country, for example, luxury goods in Poland;

- at least one that relates to the academic subject area, for example, consumer behaviour in retail purchasing;

- at least one on the particular question of interest to you, for example, to what extent the design of a store impacts on consumer perceptions of luxury goods;

- one that draws your research together and proposes something of theoretical or practical value, for example, validates a theory drawn from the literature or proposes an alteration to a business model.

How exactly you write the research objectives is a vital part of the research design. At Masters' level and beyond, the words you use to express your research become more important. Your written research objectives should use words of inquiry and analysis rather than description. We have found that it is useful to think about which verbs you are going to use to describe what you are actually going to do with your research. Bloom et al. (1956) published a classification of levels of thinking in education that is still widely used. They suggested that there were six levels of thinking ranging from the lowest, which is about collecting knowledge, through comprehension and application to analysis, synthesis, and evaluation. Lists of useful 'doing' verbs broadly apply to each level. For a Masters' dissertation, you need to show evidence of the higher levels of thinking, analysis, synthesis and evaluation. We suggest that you write research objectives that use the verbs that are appropriate for those levels of thinking (see the Suggested Activity at the end of the chapter). At postgraduate level, examiners would expect to see the inclusion and use of these verbs rather than the more descriptive verbs such as show, demonstrate, list and describe.

Practical Worked Example

So, for example, if your title or central research question was 'To what extent does the design of a store impact on consumer perceptions of luxury goods: An analysis of Polish consumer behaviour', you might start out with five or even six research objectives that are along the following lines:

- To distinguish the key characteristics of the retailing of luxury goods in Poland: This will cover some of the industry, country and business background to your study. The next objective might then relate to the academic literature on luxury goods and retailing:
- To generate from a review of the academic literature on consumer behaviour and luxury goods a list of the key variables that influence consumer perceptions in retail purchasing. You might then wish to test some of these variables by carrying out in-store and customer research in Poland.
- To design and carry out some primary research in luxury goods shops and among customers to test the extent to which these variables apply in Poland. Note that you do not need to specify in your objectives what your data collection methods are going to be.

Finally, having narrowed down your field of research to this very specific area, you would probably then want to draw wider conclusions or to make recommendations:

- to interpret the findings and draw conclusions as to the extent to which they apply to Polish luxury goods retailers; or
- to draw conclusions as to the validity of the findings in the literature, (or a particular model in the literature), in the Polish context; and/or
- to support recommendations for changes in the Polish luxury goods retailing sector.

Hypothesis and Hypotheses

Hypotheses are predictions that the researcher thinks may or may not be true in relation to the variables that have been identified and that will be tested while carrying out the research. Whilst the design and testing of hypotheses is a useful and important aspect of management research, in our experience much Masters' research is concerned with developing and exploring academic concepts and therefore hypotheses are not always necessary or desirable. Do not be worried if you do not have a hypothesis in your dissertation, even if a friend of yours has several hypotheses. A hypothesis may not be appropriate for your particular research. However if you have neither a hypothesis nor a set of research questions or objectives then you should be concerned!

Using a hypothesis to test the relationship between variables is most common in positivist research (Collis and Hussey, 2003), and you may see it in academic journal articles. A null hypothesis states that there is no relationship between the variables. It is more commonly seen in business and management research than an alternative hypothesis, which states that there is a relationship. Hypotheses are written in a specific manner with H followed by the number of the hypothesis following it. A null hypothesis has an o after the H. If using hypotheses you should follow this academic convention.

Within hypotheses there are two distinct types that you may wish to use, non-directional and directional. Non-directional hypotheses state, as in the examples below, that there is or is not a relationship, but do not specify the type of relationship. A directional hypothesis gives an 'amount' of predicted relationship, for example, 'multinational firms will be slower to develop online sales strategies than national firms' (the amount of relationship in the example is 'slower', but it could be higher, faster, more, and so on). It is also possible to combine non-directional and directional hypotheses (Creswell, 2003). You might wish to determine whether a relationship exists at all in the first place, and, if so, the amount of relationship could be tested in subsequent hypotheses. For example, H1 might be: 'A relationship exists between the age of the consumer and the rate of adoption of technology products'. Once this is or is not established, further research could be conducted to find out whether, H2, 'consumers over the age of 65 have a slower adoption rate of technology products' can be established.

These examples are not intended to be definitive 'good' examples of research topics, but the principles and steps involved could be used in developing your own questions and hypotheses. Critical to this development is the defining of key terms and variables (Collis and Hussey, 2003).

Example 1

An MBA student who works in the service sector decides to research 'first movers and success in service industries'.

Step 1 – Define your key variables

In this case, key variables are first movers and success (and the elements that make up that success, or those that will be a focus of the research) and service industries.

Step 2 – Decide whether you wish to develop a hypothesis to test or a research question

Decisions about writing research questions or hypotheses will be based on what type of research you are undertaking, inductive (phenomenological) or deductive (positivist) and also what types of research design you feel more comfortable with. In addition, what outcome you expect, as well as the subject area itself may shape the research question formulation.

Step 3 – Turn into question form or a hypothesis

The research question could be: 'What happens to first movers in service industries?'

However, if you wished to develop a hypothesis to test, it could be written as: 'There is a relationship between a service company that offers a new service and market share or profitability or sales growth and so on'.

A null hypothesis would be written as: 'There is no relationship between a service company that offers a new service and …'

Example 2

An MSc student says: 'I want to research mergers and acquisitions in the pharmaceutical industry, and the impact on their over-the-counter (OTC) drug business'.

Step 1 – Define the variables

In this case, the variables are mergers and acquisitions, OTC drugs and the speed of commercialization of new drugs.

Step 2 – Decide whether

You wish to develop a hypothesis to test or a research question.

Step 3 – Turn into question form or a hypothesis.
A question could be:
Does a merger or acquisition affect the speed of commercialization of OTC drugs?'

A hypothesis could be:
'There is a relationship between mergers and acquisitions activity and the rate of OTC drug commercialization.'

Getting Access

If you are relying on collecting primary data to answer some of your research questions, it is really important to work out how you will get access to the organizations or individuals you wish to use in your research. Members of organizations limit the time available for interviews, lose your questionnaires, go on holiday, change jobs in the middle of your data collection schedule or simply block access to information. People may make promises about giving information to students that they have little intention of fulfilling. In order to protect your own interests, you must make a realistic assessment of how you will get access to an organization or to primary data. Use the self-check questions in the box below. Be ruthless – if you do not expect too much you may be pleasantly surprised, but it can be fatal to be over-optimistic at the beginning.

Self check questions on access

* **Who will grant it?**

* **Can I get confirmation over the phone or preferably in writing or by email before I start my research?**

* **When?**

* **What terms will they impose?**

* **Will they let me use the results in my dissertation?**

There are a number of strategies you can use to improve your chances of getting access. The first is obvious – start early – because it can take ages to organize. Try and use existing contacts and from them develop new ones, so that you develop your access bit by bit. It is important to use the right language and to establish your credibility as a researcher. Try to create a good impression. Do dress appropriately and make it easy for the people you wish to speak to, to contact you. Make a virtue of the fact that you are a genuine student, for example use university-headed note paper or a university email address rather than your joke hotmail name or term-time accommodation address. Describe exactly what you want to do and what it is for. If possible, try to identify possible benefits to the organization or individual in giving you access. But do be realistic about the amount of help you can offer – you are doing it for yourself in the first instance. This applies even if what you are doing is a work-based project or piece of consultancy for a higher business diploma or degree. The academic requirements of the institution that is awarding you the qualification must come first.

Time

You must make sure that you know how long your project will take to research and how long it will take to write up. You need to write a time chart. Divide up the time between when you plan to start work on it and the date for submission into meaningful segments and attach some milestones to each. You can hand draw this or do it on a computer. Milestones can be key events or stages in your research, such as the date for pilot testing a questionnaire, or a date by which you will have transcribed your interviews. Do try to be realistic about what you can and can't do. If you are too optimistic about early progress, you may get very discouraged. Most people tend to speed up as they get further in to their research and more expert at it. Within each time period, you need to be fairly sure of what you can achieve on a week-by-week basis. Don't forget to include on your chart family events, planned holidays and periods such as religious festivals when you are unlikely to do any work. We suggest that you send your chart to family members and close friends, as well as your supervisor, so that people around you can see the level of commitment you are making to your research project or dissertation. It might help to both keep you going and also to discourage distractions. Once you have actually started, you can of course revise your timetable – in fact it is important that you do so – so that it stays realistic.

Towards the middle of your time, you should be able to make a reasonably accurate chart of remaining tasks and to allot the time required. Then all you have to do is to try and stick to it. If you find yourself getting seriously behind, you should try to find out why. Were you just over optimistic, about how fast you can read, for example? Is the scope of your project much bigger than you realized? Are the boundaries you set at the outset in the right place? You may at some stage need to scale down or reassess your research objectives and the initial boundaries you set to your research so that you can finish your dissertation in the time allotted for it.

Writing your Research Proposal

You will probably be asked by your course tutors to write a research proposal that may form part of your assessment. Check your course regulations carefully as to what your course tutors suggest should go into your research proposal, as different institutions have different requirements. Below we give some suggestions as to what it is likely to include, and an example of a research proposal for a 20 000–word dissertation for an MSc in International Management.

Suggested research proposal content

A working title for your project or dissertation

This working title should enable a reader or your supervisor to quickly grasp the focus of your research. Working titles often evolve over the period of research into something that is rather different from what you started with – you shouldn't worry about this, but you should aim to make your first attempt at a title as clear and straightforward as possible. Your working title should encapsulate the purpose of the project. Clarity in the title will also help you to focus and to structure all the research and reading that you do later. At this stage, being clear is more important than being witty! Many students find it helps to write their working title as a question that sums up what they are trying to find out in their dissertation. A good check of whether you have come up with a reasonable working title is to pretend that you have met someone for the first time and that they ask you what your dissertation is on. Can you express it clearly in one sentence? That should be your working title.

A statement of your key research questions or objectives

In a research proposal, you would be expected to include a brief explanation of how you have arrived at your research objectives, research questions and/or hypotheses and what they are. Some institutions are quite prescriptive about whether you write research questions or research objectives and you should do whichever is required. You should try to show the links between your working title, what you wish to find out and how you have expressed this as questions/objectives and hypotheses (Collis and Hussey, 2003).

A section that describes the background to the subject

This section should be in the form of a brief description of the background to a particular business sector, for example automobile manufacturing, or a specific company such as British Airways, or a specific policy such as the enlargement of the EU. Only relevant material should be included to give the reader confidence that you understand the context in which you are going to carry out your research, and that you are aware of a few key sources.

A section that demonstrates that you know who the key authors in your field are

At the time of writing the proposal you would not be expected to know and to have read every relevant author in your chosen field. However, you should show that you are aware of who the leading academic business authors are on your topic and where your research will fit with their ideas. This section will eventually form the basis of your literature search and subsequent review of the academic literature.

A case that argues why it is worth doing at all

Your research proposal is actually an academic selling document. You are trying to sell your research idea to your supervisor and proposal assessor and therefore you need to justify why your project is worth doing. Personal interest in a subject can be mentioned, but the point here is to be able to explain the potential value of your project, not to bare your soul. For example, might it add insight for management decision-making? Might the outcome be an enhanced model that could be applied and tested in future research?

An outline of your chosen research methods

You will need to have a clear idea how you will conduct your research before you start it. Your research methods underpin your research objectives or questions, as they are the means by which you expect to find out the answers to the questions or to achieve the objectives. You should include an overview of why a certain approach will be taken or why you have chosen certain methods (Collis and Hussey, 2003) as well as an outline of whether and why you will use secondary research or primary or both. The methods for data collection you intend to use should be appropriate to the type of research you are undertaking. For example, if you were undertaking primary research, deciding to use questionnaires to ask people how they feel about fairness of pay across a company would not be entirely appropriate. You might not get very honest or sensible answers. You would want people to define what they meant by 'fair', for example, as it might mean different things to different people. This could be difficult in a survey. A better method might be to consider the use of focus groups, each one containing only the same level or pay grade of employees, to encourage open dialogue. This could perhaps be followed by individual interviews. Referring to at least one of the specialist textbooks on research methods will help guide your choices. In your proposal, you should also try to indicate which methods may provide data to answer specific objectives or questions. You also need to give a realistic assessment of your ability to carry out your research. If it is to be based on interviews of chief executives, for example, you need to show that you will definitely be able to get access to these people.

Resources and constraints

This section should deal with the practicalities of how you will use your resources and what might hinder your project. Time management needs to be made explicit by drawing a timeline or writing down when you plan to do each part of your dissertation, with paid employment, holidays and family commitments factored in to the schedule. You need to remember that while July and August might be good months for you, at least in the northern hemisphere the people you want to speak to may well be on holiday. Financial constraints should also be outlined. Can you afford to conduct face-to-face interviews in different parts of the country or even to fly abroad to do your research?

Research ethics

Many institutions require you to consider any ethical issues that might arise from your research and to include this with your research proposal. Even if they do not make it a formal requirement that your research proposal covers this, you should still consider it. People have a human right not to be researched and if your research involves primary data collection involving people – which most business research does – then you have a duty to make sure that people's dignity, privacy and confidences are respected, and that any data you collect, particularly anything that identifies any one, is handled correctly. Fortunately, doing business research is not as intrusive as research in medicine or psychology, but you do need to be aware that asking questions about, for example, people's job roles can be upsetting for those taking part in your research, and that people have a right to refuse to answer your questions, to refuse to take part in your research and to withdraw their consent to participate in it at a later date. In business research particularly, you need to be very careful not to betray things people have told you in confidence to others and to disguise their identities when you write up your research if they have asked you to do so.

In your research proposal you should also note any other areas that might prove problematic. For example, if your project depends on gaining access to a particular company, what might happen if permission is not granted? Do you need specific books and will these be available to you when you need them? Might you have to buy some key texts if they are not available from a library? Are there internal organizational boundaries that might be difficult to cross in your research? If you are trying to research a contentious issue such as staff retention, performance related pay or hostile take-overs as an employee of the organization under scrutiny, then trying to conduct internal research could prove difficult, not to mention potentially damaging for your career progression within that organization. You must also make sure that you comply with any rules your institution has on the collection and storage of personal data and any legislation on data handling and data privacy.

References

A list of references must be part of your proposal and you should follow whichever referencing system your institution prefers, and use it consistently throughout all your work. Remember that a reference list is used for those materials you have cited in the text and a bibliography is used for materials which may be relevant to the topic you are researching but have not actually, specifically used. You may well have both in your proposal.

Once you have written and submitted your proposal, you should have a clearer sense of your dissertation. Although it seems quite a lot of work early on, the more detail and depth you can give in your proposal, the more straightforward the process of your research will be.

Example MSc Research Proposal

Below is an example of an MSc research proposal presentation for a dissertation using secondary data.

Working title:

- **Is luxury branding global?**

Background/context:

- **the growing importance of branding;**

- **the increase in sales of luxury goods internationally;**

- **whether luxury branding should be global in its application;**

- **value of adding to limited knowledge on this growing marketing topic.**

(Why is it worth researching this area?)

Academic context:

- **main globalization authors – Hankinson, Keegan, Levitt, Yip, Ramarupu;**

- **main luxury goods authors – Dubois, Berry, Roux;**

- main branding authors – Kapferer, Aaker, Temporal;

- main consumption authors – Bourdieu, McCracken.

(How do these fit together?)

Research objectives:

- to analyse the literature on brand management;

- to distinguish the characteristics of international luxury brand management;

- to determine whether generalizations made from existing research on luxury brand management are relevant for a non-western culture.

(What do you really want to find out?)

Methods:

- main secondary sources – textbooks such as *The New Strategic Brand Management* by Kapferer (2004), *Journal of Product and Brand Management*, other international journals on marketing and consumption;

- sources from own university library, other libraries, academic journal databases, British library inter-library loans;

- collated under the main themes of my objectives, then broken down into sub-themes;

- appraise the arguments and evidence of the authors collected.

(How am I going to collect, collate and appraise the material?)

Timescale and constraints

- Read and prepare proposal for 20 February deadline.

- February–April: collect relevant literature and make notes, alter working title if necessary.

- **26 March–4 April: Easter holiday.**

- **May–June: continue with literature search and begin writing.**

- **July: start writing outcome and summary of literature review.**

- **End July: draft to supervisor.**

- **End August–early September: make revisions.**

- **16 September: final submission.**

References
Kapferer, J-N. (2004) *The New Strategic Brand Management*. London: Kogan Page.
McCracken, G. (1986) 'Culture and consumption: A theoretical account of the structure and movement of the cultural meaning of consumer goods', *Journal of Consumer Research*, 13(1): 71–84.

Note: This is for illustrative purposes only – you would have many more.

Practical Worked Example

An MSc Research Proposal for a Dissertation in International Management

This is based on an actual dissertation proposal for a successfully completed dissertation.

Working title

Which market entry strategies would be most appropriate for an ambitious service company based in one emerging market and seeking to move into others within the EU?

Background

In anticipation of the enlargement of the EU, many businesses have recognized the need to assess the potential impacts as well as to seize opportunities and to deal with any potential threats that may arise. After assessing the situation in the emerging markets of the EU, in particular Poland and the Baltic states, it became apparent that there is a significant difference between the EU newcomers and the existing member states in the market research sector. Particularly striking in the emerging markets is the lack of publicly available market research reports, when compared with the rest of the EU. Those that are available seem to be of very limited coverage and of questionable quality. These factors might signify a significant gap in the provision of market research services and the possibility of future demand potential for these services.

Currently, there are only a few players in the market research sector in these emerging markets. Most of the companies provide only limited research in response to individual client requests, which is supplied only to the customer and is not published. Such services are extremely expensive and usually inaccessible for local small-to-medium enterprises (SMEs). In Poland, there is some publicly available research on the main local industries, but in the Baltic states there is almost none. A recent trawl by the author found, for example, that in Latvia there were only a couple of market research reports and these had a very narrow focus. It seems that some specific companies may have made even these available for promotion purposes, so their authority and independence is questionable.

The main focus of the study will be to test the applicability of theoretical concepts about market entry strategies to an SME (focusing on one market research company, XYZ) entering the emerging markets of Europe (focusing on Poland and the Baltic states). XYZ company will be used as an example to illustrate the theoretical framework as well as practical issues.

Academic context

Before the author is in a position to provide any meaningful recommendations to XYZ and to draw conclusions valid for SMEs in a similar position, the underpinning theories and concepts relating to market entry will be thoroughly examined and critically evaluated. These academic models, frameworks and concepts, if used in a critical and intelligent way, allow for a much better analysis and understanding of the situation in hand, when applied to a practical context. They could also act as a checklist to ensure no important variables were overlooked in the decision-making process.

By looking at this topic from an academic perspective, several supporting key academic ideas can be identified. The first of these is the concept of market entry, which was defined by Bradley as relating to 'the ease or difficulty with which a firm can become a member of a group of competing firms by producing a close substitute for the products they are offering' (Bradley, 1991: 323)

example continues

example continues

For most companies, the most significant international marketing decision they have to make is which new markets to enter and how they should do it. Koch (2001) divides major market entry decisions into:

- choice of a target/product market;
- timing of entry;
- choice of an entry mode;
- objectives and goals in the target market;
- marketing plan to penetrate the market;
- the control systems needed to monitor performance.

The main academic ideas on market selection come from authors such as Williamson (1985) on market entry mode, and Toyne and Walters (1989) on the host countries' political, economic, social and technological environment. Additionally, studies on entry timing have been done by Gilbert (1993). More general international business marketing studies include those by Hofstede (1994), and the importance of monitoring the process of market entry is recognized by many authors, for instance Kotler (1997).

Research objectives

The ultimate purpose of this dissertation is to apply academic knowledge and tools derived from the literature on market entry strategies to specific market conditions in order to develop a practical framework for XYZ and to provide them with recommendations that are firmly grounded in academic literature. The above can be split into the following research objectives:

1   to review and critically evaluate the academic literature on international market entry with a particular emphasis on SMEs and potential barriers to entry;
2   to distinguish the specific market characteristics in Poland and the Baltic states that affect a potential entrant to the market research sector;
3   to examine the competitive landscape in Poland and the Baltic states and identify barriers to entry in the market research sector;
4   to analyse XYZ's actions so far in regard to market entry strategies and assess them in the light of academic theories and models;
5   to support recommendations for XYZ on possible further steps, especially as regards how they might overcome identified entry barriers;
6   to draw conclusions as to the extent to which the academic literature is applicable to the experience of SMEs in these markets.

Research methods and access

The research approach should be decided by the nature of the research topic (Creswell, 2003). In this particular situation, the research question is ultimately how to penetrate the Polish and Baltic markets for market research reporting, by adopting effective market entry strategies. Many scholars have already researched market entry strategies, and the aim is to build on that. The most suitable approach, therefore, seems to be deductive research, as I am trying to verify already developed academic concepts in a real business setting, rather than to develop a new framework or theory.

Secondary data

In order to satisfy the research objectives, a thorough review of the available literature on the subject of market entry strategies will be undertaken. The author has already identified a preliminary reading list (copy attached [not included here]) on which all the literature identified is available in the university library in hard copy or electronic form. As the reading progresses and the scope of the research become more defined, further reading needs will be identified and met.

Secondary data is data that already exists and there is a variety of sources available to a researcher (Saunders et al., 2003). The most challenging part of the secondary data collection will be to examine the external environment for the market research industry in these countries, as there is no market research available on the market research industry in these countries. Research on the following elements will therefore need to be undertaken:

- competitor analysis – using Datamonitor, Euromonitor and the Internet, and so on, to identify current key players and potential entrants from elsewhere in the EU;
- using other publicly available data information sources such as government publications and newspapers to assess the extent of their coverage and their potential use for business decision-making;
- analysing the projected impact of EU enlargement on these emerging markets from published sources, of which there is a vast amount available.

In addition, access to some Polish, Latvian, Lithuanian, and Estonian databases online will be purchased in order to enable the author to review articles on the researched subject published in major newspapers and journals in those countries.

example continues

example continues

To satisfy the dissertation's objectives fully, it will be worthwhile to carry out some primary research, in order to gain 'a rich understanding of the context of the research and the processes being enacted' (Morris and Wood, 1991 quoted in Saunders et al., 2003: 94). In order to generate answers to questions such as 'how' or 'why?', some authors advise a case study approach (Robson, 1993) and argue that 'a case study can be a very worthwhile way of exploring existing theory' (Saunders et al., 2003: 94). That is why a company has been selected in order to act as an example or case study and to provide some primary data for the dissertation.

Primary data

Primary data is that data which is collected specifically for the project by the researcher. It can be gathered by a number of means. For the purpose of assessing XYZ company's internal environment, access to the company has been agreed in order to carry out interviews with employees and to examine company records.

An interview is 'a purposeful discussion between two or more people' (Kahn and Cannell, 1957 quoted in Saunders et al., 2003: 242). Interviews in this instance seem to be most appropriate in order to study and understand the internal environment of the organization (decision-making, resources, intentions, culture, and so on). The flexibility of an interview allows for in-depth questions and spontaneous variations, depending on the flow of the conversation. There are several types of interview, which vary in the level of their formality and their structure. The author plans to conduct 10 one-to-one, face-to-face, semi-structured interviews (with about half the total staff of XYZ), including managers and employees, as they are considered to be 'information rich' sources (Krueger and Casey, 2002). The interviews will be semi-structured because this non-standardized approach will facilitate an exploration of the complexity of the topic (Saunders et al., 2003: 251) with a list of themes and questions used to form the basis of the interview. A completely unstructured interview is considered inappropriate for this project, as it is does not provide the necessary framework for the discussion (Saunders et al., 2003: 243–4).

The company interviews will enable the author to obtain first-hand information on the structure, processes, resources and strategies of the company. It might also be possible to gain valuable information from the development agencies established in all four countries (there is one in each of Poland, Latvia, Lithuania and Estonia). The author believes they play a big role in the local markets in knowledge sharing and the provision of market information. He will therefore approach them in order to gain data. However, there is no guarantee that they will share this information. To maximize the chances of success, it is crucial that face-to-face interviews are undertaken where possible. Due to budgetary constraints, it will be possible only to travel to Latvia and interviews over the telephone will be attempted with the other three countries.

Research ethics

XYZ company has agreed to give full access to the company's internal (confidential) data. Furthermore, an assurance was given that employees of the company will give their support provided that it does not interfere with their duty to the company. However, certain conditions have to be met by the author. They are:

- non-disclosure of the company name in published material – therefore a false company name will be used in the dissertation;
- non-disclosure of some employee names – their names will be replaced by numbers in the reports on the primary data collection;
- a signed confidentiality agreement between the author and XYZ;
- the final report should be kept confidential and not disclosed – I have shown them the Business School's confidentiality policy and they have accepted it;
- all published material should be shared with the company – but they have agreed that they will not request any respondent-specific information and that interview replies will be confidential to the researcher and the interviewee.
- to minimize psychological pressure on interviewees, they will be informed about the academic purpose of the research, and that they do not have to participate, do not have to answer any question they do not wish to answer, and can end the interview at any time.
- completed research ethics checklist attached [not included here].

Timescale and resources

[A detailed plan was included listing all the activities broken down by duration, location and the deadline for finishing them.]

References

[Full list of references in Harvard format, not included here.]

Summary

This chapter has dealt with how to move your research ideas from being ideas to achievable objectives and questions. It has included a brief guide to devising hypotheses and research questions and to what constitutes a research proposal. You should now be able to state what you wish to find out as objectives in questions or in hypothesis form. The more clearly you state your questions, the more straightforward it will be to design research to find answers to your questions. The questions you ask must be answerable within the constraints of the degree you are aiming for. At Masters' level, you are expected to research a narrow area in depth and this necessitates careful construction of the research questions. Practical matters such as gaining access and time management are often neglected, and are important to get right.

Suggested Activity

Writing Your Research Objectives

Look at the learning map you created at the end of Chapter 3 and try to write a draft set of research objectives. Try to use some of the verbs suggested below developed from Bloom's taxonomy (Bloom et al., 1956) if you get stuck. Try to write a maximum of five and make them feasible, bearing in mind any constraints you may have (time, money, company limitations). When you have done this, leave your draft set and come back to them the next day, re-read them and assess how achievable they really are. You may have to amend your original attempt.

Using Bloom et al.'s (1956) Taxonomy of useful 'doing' words

Analysis:	analyse, categorize, criticize, differentiate, distinguish, examine, question, test
Synthesis:	compile, contrast, construct, create, design, generate, organize, plan, propose
Evaluation:	appraise, assess, compare, estimate, evaluate, interpret, judge, justify, predict, rate, support

Discussion Questions

1 Why is writing a research proposal considered essential to the research process?

2 What is your interpretation of a positioning statement?

3 Can you outline the differences between a research question and a hypothesis?

Further Reading

Punch, K. (2000) *Developing Effective Research Proposals.* **London: Sage.** There are chapters in many research methods textbooks on how to write research proposals. An excellent short book on the subject is:

Creswell, J.W. (2003) *Research Design: Qualitative, Quantitative, and Mixed Methods Approaches* **(2nd edition). London: Sage.** This goes into the whole issue of research design in much greater depth than the more general texts – a useful reference source.

5 Sources of Secondary Information

How Do I Know If I Should Include It?

The aim of this chapter is to help you to learn how to identify the appropriate areas of literature for your assignments and dissertation. You can spend a lot of time reading and collecting secondary information that turns out to be worthless, so it is important to develop your skills to assess it in advance for its rigour and value.

Secondary Data

Using secondary data in your assignment or dissertation can be defined as 're-analysing data collected already for some other purpose', as well as published summaries of that data. Basically, secondary information is all the data that has been collected by others but is available to you as a student of business and management. Whatever you are working on for an assignment or dissertation, you are bound to need to look at some secondary data. This chapter covers the types and relative value of different sources of secondary information, including the Internet and its uses and abuses, and when and how to use newspaper sources and trade journals, as well as the value of secondary data in general.

Whether you are writing coursework or for a dissertation, one key criterion for a good piece of work is that you draw on a 'wide range' of secondary literature. There is no problem in finding it – the Internet gives you access to vast resources undreamed of by earlier generations of students. The problem thus rapidly comes down to what to include and what to exclude, and how to make sense of it all.

Types of secondary data

In an effort to make it more manageable, various authors of textbooks on research methods try to distinguish different categories of secondary information. Saunders et al. (2003) distinguish three types, which they categorize as documentary, multiple source, and survey data. By documentary, they mean both written documents, such as organizational records and academics' notes, and non-written materials such as television programmes. They distinguish all this from survey data, which is the published, or at least accessible, results of surveys in the form of quantitative, mainly questionnaire-based, studies done by other organizations. A national census is a good example of this. Their final category is what they describe as 'multiple source data', which is a mixture of the two, for example, many government publications and country reports (Saunders et al., 2003).

Other authors (for example McGivern, 2003) refer simply to internal sources of data and external sources. This is really only relevant for an MBA or DMS student who is doing research in their own organization and so has excellent access to internal sources of data such as company records and in-house databases. Secondary data in this context can include any data the company has collected. That might include accounting information, sales data and figures on returned goods, sales force data, personnel records, electronic point of sale data, and other management information that has been systematically collected in the course of doing business. It can be a really valuable source of information. Analysing the records made by salespeople, of who and where they visited and what these particular customers ordered, can reveal fascinating and revealing insights into how customers perceive that particular company. Personnel records, if access to them is possible, can provide revealing data on a range of human resource issues.

Although it is important to be aware of all the different types of secondary information, for the purposes of your written work, the key distinction might just be the difference between 'secondary data in general' and that part of it that eventually might form part of the literature review chapter or chapters of your dissertation. We have found with our students that for the purposes of a dissertation, you can treat secondary data as forming two potential final outputs:

- **Academic 'stuff', which is derived mainly from books and academic journals and is written up in the literature review part of your dissertation. Most assignments will also contain a section on the academic background or literature. The central purpose of your literature review is to meet the academic requirements of your dissertation and to help you to build a critical framework for analysing the**

- **'Other stuff', which may comprise all your other secondary data *and* the results of your primary data collection.**

This chapter is mainly about how you collect and analyse the secondary data that forms 'the other stuff', but it should be read alongside Chapter 6, which is on critical reading and mainly about the 'academic stuff', because it is necessary, indeed vital, to develop a critical approach to both.

There are considerable advantages to using secondary data as part of any assignment or dissertation. An obvious one is that such data can cover much longer time periods than most researchers could otherwise manage. Secondary data enables researchers to get access to contemporaneously collected data from the past, which is now impossible to collect. You can read newspaper reports and company reports from 1995 instead of having to rely on what people remember today about what happened in that year. It may be subject to less bias as a result. Secondary information enables you to get interviews – albeit at second hand – with individuals such as chief executives, whom in the normal course of events it would be impossible to reach. The Managing Director of Unilever is most unlikely to grant you an exclusive interview about the company's brand strategy, but will talk to the *Financial Times* or the trade press when the company results are due. You can then analyse that reported interview. That is one reason why newspapers, and business and trade magazines can be such important sources of information.

Some authors also argue that because secondary data has already been collected, it is non-reactive and as a result there is less interviewer or researcher bias and the combined expertise and experience of those who collected it can make it very high quality (Bryman and Bell, 2003). The problem, of course, is that the purpose for which the information was collected originally may not match your need now. You also have to rely on some-one else's perception of what should have been measured or recorded. Unfortunately, you have no control over the outcomes, and any inherent biases in the original data collection may be hidden and are difficult to take account of. It is also difficult to test for competing explanations using a data set that can't be collected in a different way or altered. In any dissertation that relies on *secondary* data collection, these problems must be discussed in the methodology section and allowed for in the research design.

It is not difficult to find a lot of secondary data on most business topics. The main problems lie in deciding where to start, where to go next, how you know you are looking in the right place and when you know you can stop. Another important issue to consider is what records you have to keep.

An Approach to Collecting your Secondary Information Systematically

Where to start

It is a good idea to start by looking at the requirements of your course, module, assignment and dissertation. In some universities they can be very specific, even specifying for particular assignments the number and type of source you are expected to use. At the same time, you have to remember that postgraduate courses themselves have certain expectations that students will meet higher standards of rigour and critical understanding than at undergraduate or certificate level. For an MBA and DMS student, rigour must be shown in the way you address both a practical management issue and demonstrate a thorough grounding in theory. For an MA or MSc student in business and management, most courses do not expect a practical knowledge of the subject. Rigour is to do with demonstrating that you have a thorough grounding in academic literature and theory and that you could then apply it to a practical management problem.

The best place to start collecting your secondary information is not by looking on the World Wide Web, nor in your workplace, but in your university or college library. It sounds too obvious to write down, but in our experience many students rush straight to the Internet search engines, forgetting about the university library altogether. There are two very good reasons for starting in the library. The first is that the university library should be seen as a giant sieve or filtration plant. Everything that is in there has been included for a sound academic reason. This can be enormously helpful, particularly when you compare it with the World Wide Web, where there is no filtration system. Not all of what you find in the library will by any means be brilliant or even particularly good, but the real rubbish will never have been put there in the first place. The second great virtue of academic libraries is that they are organized and catalogued in a logical fashion, with the books grouped together by subject speciality, and sub-speciality, and then alphabetically by author's surname. On any business topic, it makes considerable sense to exhaust all non-Internet 'local' print resources *before* you start online. This makes it really easy to get a quick overview of who the key authors are in a subject area and what are the most closely related topics.

Simply browsing the library shelves can be enormously helpful in the early stages of data collection. If you have really no idea where to begin, start with the library shelf or shelves that contain the books on the research topic area you are interested in. Note how they are subdivided using the decimal system, so that 658 breaks down into 658.1, 658.2, 658.3 and so on and then 658.3, for example, is further subdivided. For example, 658.8 is marketing and within this you can find 658.8002–Internet marketing; 658.8007 marketing case studies; 658.80094 marketing in European countries; 658.0095 marketing in Japan; 658.802 not-for-profit marketing; 658.81 sales management, and so on. Thus the large numbers indicate the subject area and the subsequent smaller numbers show the subsection within that subject area. You can also browse the library shelves by using the library's online catalogue. It will of course include books that are out on loan and so not currently on the shelf, which can be very helpful at certain peak periods when many of the books are out on loan. Click on the shelf mark you want and use the navigation tools to browse for other titles with the same shelf mark. You can also search under key words from the titles of books if you don't know exactly what you are searching for, for example, product development. Then go to the library to have a look at what is there.

Pick some of the books from the shelves and select a few, starting with those that have been first published most recently. Discard anything that is more than 7 years old unless you have a very good reason to read it – business and management is a very fast-moving subject. Information on when the book was first published is normally on the back of the title page. It should not take you too long to identify a few key authors. Look up the references, which will be listed at the end of chapters or together at the back, and at the footnotes in a couple of these books. They will lead you to others, and into the main academic journals associated with your topic area.

Academic journal articles provide you with the most up-to-date thinking in universities on your topic area. You must get to grips with them, as they will enable you to demonstrate in your dissertation that you are familiar with the latest academic thinking on a subject. Few universities can afford to subscribe to all the academic journals in each subject area, particularly in business and management, where the subject is so vast and diverse. However, you should start with the ones that your library does take, before branching out into those that are available electronically. See Chapter 6 for how to spot what an academic journal looks like – they are sometimes shelved alongside business and trade magazines, so it is not always obvious. It is still much easier on the eye and the brain to browse through bound volumes of journals than to do it all electronically. Also, you should be able to assume that the ones that your library takes in print form are the ones that they regard as the most essential. Start by going through the indexes or contents pages of the bound volumes of the leading academic journals in your subject area for the last 5 years (the current year will of course not be bound yet). You may well pick up articles that you would never otherwise have found by searching electronically. Academic research is full of sidetracks and interesting turnings that may lead to dead ends, but could also be fascinating and open up whole new aspects of the subject for you to explore. Use this as an opportunity to investigate some of these. They may lead you in some very interesting directions.

Where to go next

It is vitally important to show that you can take a critical and sceptical approach to *all* written materials, wherever you find them (see Chapter 6 for how to develop an effective approach to critical reading). This is even more crucial when you have finished in the university library and start to look at what is available on the World Wide Web. The impact of the huge growth and development of electronic sources on secondary data collection has been immense. Business and management students, in particular, are faced with the very real problem of information overload and it can sometimes be quite disheartening to find out how much information there is available on your research topic, as you are faced with the huge problem of categorizing, weighing and sorting it – and of throwing quite a lot out. The Internet gives access to a far wider range of information of much more variable quality than that found in university libraries, and you need to develop your skills to work out the credibility and the authority of documents you find there. You need your own filtration system.

In order to start on a web-based search, you need to use a search engine. A search engine is just a tool – some are better at looking for certain things on the web than others, but there tends to be a lack of consistency in results. Most academics use Google™ (www.google.co.uk), and many use nothing else. If you are having difficulty tracking something down, it is a good idea to try several different search engines to see how the results vary. Popular alternatives to Google include WebFetch (www.webfetch.com) (the new name for Dogpile), Meta4 (www.meta4.com) and AllSearch Engines (www.allsearchengines.co.uk) There are many other non-academic search engines available to you via the web. These broader engines can point you in the right direction and provide some background information that may assist you in narrowing your topic area. Some of these engines can be helpful but many others come and go.

Most academic libraries now have access to a vast range of dedicated web-based academic databases that they subscribe to, or that are provided through central university library funding. Go to your academic library home page and find the link to their electronic journals. You will probably need to register online in order to do this. You can search the journals using a keyword for the title of the journal, so, for instance, if you are looking for something on brands, you could turn up all the journals with the word 'brand' in their title. Then the database will let you know how to access that particular journal electronically.

The most commonly available journal databases in British universities that are used for business and management research are: EBSCO (www.ebsco.com), which hosts several databases, the most important for business students being Business Source Premier, and EconLit. Business Source Premier contains hundreds of full-text journals and abstracts in management, business and economics and company, industry and country reports too. EconLit is a comprehensive bibliography with citations and abstracts of the world's economic literature produced by the American Economic Association. Emerald has full text and abstracts of 120 journals published by MCB University Press. It is particularly strong in certain subject areas such as marketing. Zetoc (zetoc.mimas.ac.uk) is an academic database available in British universities. It is produced by the British Library and carries references – only – to articles from the 20 000 most important research journals in the world, including business journals, and over 100 000 conference papers. Your institution may subscribe to different academic databases, so check with your subject librarian or their web pages. Other academic databases include SOSIG and BIDS.

There are many other academic and business databases that you may find very helpful. Business Insight (previously Reuters), provides international market and business reports on consumer markets, finance, energy, pharmaceuticals and technology; Euromonitor contains market research reports on UK, European and world markets, and reports on world retail sectors; Mintel has UK market research reports on consumer goods, leisure, and retailing; Thomson Gale (previously Infotrac) is the host for Investext, which contains in-depth analysts' reports on companies, industries, markets and countries, and for PROMT, which contains news items on companies, markets, industries and products from 1000 world newspapers and trade journals. These should be regarded as useful sources of published data – but you should use them as a basis for further data manipulation and analysis, rather than simply copying the information they present.

Databases that contain articles from major newspapers and the business press are very useful information sources. Proquest Newspapers' database (proquest.umi.com) provides the full text (but not photographs or graphics) of 32 UK newspapers including all quality national newspapers. Usually text is available the day after publication. UK quality papers dating back to 1995–96 and the full text of the *Financial Times* back to 1996 are available. Most business libraries also subscribe to the *Economist* (www.economist. com) database.

These databases cover a very wide spectrum from economics and financial company data to broader sector information and also specific academic research articles as well as some consultancy reports. Sadly they all have slightly differing search systems, so be prepared to spend time honing your searching skills. Do not be put off by the message 'no articles match your search'; just try again using different terms of reference or a different database.

For example, a search for material on 'brand management' using two different databases came up with the following results. Using Proquest, 165 results were found. These ranged from newspaper articles with just the phrase 'brand management' mentioned once, to a *Financial Times* article focusing on current brand management issues. When the database was filtered to only include scholarly rather than newspaper or trade magazine articles, there was only one result, a 1996 article in the *Journal of Health Care Marketing*. This might have been a rather disappointing result depending on what data was needed. However, Proquest is where you should look for newspaper reports and that is most likely in this context to be company news. It is not a good place to try and find academic articles because it contains so few.

The second search, which was conducted on the Emerald database, gave 574 results for academic journal articles on 'brand management'. If you were searching for academic articles to use for your literature review, then Emerald would have been a useful tool for you, and one that is available at many universities. You could reduce the 574 articles by setting limits on the date of publication, for example, nothing before 1998, or by only selecting certain authors, for example, Kapferer. However, if you had tried to search Emerald by putting in a company name then, unlike with Proquest, you would be unlikely to have had many 'hits', as Emerald is purely an academic journal article database. There are many other databases and unfortunately their names and the publications that they cover change frequently. It is worth asking your tutors and friends for useful search engine recommendations.

Once you have tried a few search engines, you will have an amazing amount of potential documents to work with, but the real problem is how to assess the extent to which they are likely to be helpful to you. You can spend hours looking at each one, a process that can be very frustrating and time consuming with little positive result. Working with our students, and using as a starting point a book by O' Dochartaigh (2003), on which this section is largely based, we have established a hierarchy of reliability for web-based resources for research in business and management, reproduced below. It is unfortunately not always easy to recognize which of these categories a particular site may fall into. O' Dochartaigh provides some useful advice and tips on this in his book.

A hierarchy of reliability of web-based resources for business and management students

- **Academic documents – for example, journal articles, and academic web pages, are your most reliable potential source, but it is vital that you know how to recognize them, and how to distinguish those that are of the highest quality. The domain names you need to look for are .edu or .ac, but many academic journal articles are only available on closed subscription online databases. It is difficult to give general guidance on this because different universities subscribe to different online services. You need to check with your university or college library as to which ones are available to you. Make a point of using them first before starting a search on the open web. For more on journal articles, see Chapter 6.**

- **Official documents – these can be rich sources, particularly of country data, but they are almost always very one-sided. Government websites will try to present the rosiest picture possible of their home country. There are good reasons for this – they are trying to attract overseas investors or tourists to visit the country. Governments also try to manage their news, so that the politicians in charge appear in the best possible light. Government press releases can provide useful summaries of reports but will be designed to give the government a favourable image. Favourite tricks can include publishing documents on government websites without a press announcement, or issuing a lot of documents on the same day or on a public holiday in the hope that they will not be much noticed, or publishing documents when the national parliament is not in session. You may have to** hunt around the more obscure corners of government websites to find reports and documents that they have been obliged to publish but are not particularly proud of. National governments are the most reliable sources of statistical data, but even then they attempt to present the good news. Try always to go back to the raw data if at all possible rather than relying on news releases of selected statistics. This may mean that you have to visit the specialist national statistical office website in each country rather than the website of one government department.

- News documents – these are produced by organizations whose business is to sell news. They can and will be political, partisan, inaccurate and one-sided. At the same time they may be all you can find, particularly if you are trying to look at the development of a business practice or organization over a period of time. You must treat all news reports with extreme caution. Try to look in several newspaper archives for reports on the same event. Different newspapers and business magazines will have their own slant. Note any similarities: it could be an indication that it all comes from one company press release or briefing. How 'objective' is it? It is always refreshing to look at the foreign press reports and to compare what they have to say with what the main news media in a country are saying about a particular event or business in that country.

- The trade press – this is a potentially helpful source, as it consists of specialist magazines devoted to information about one business sector or trade. A lot is available online through online databases, for example, Business Source Premier contains trade journals alongside academic ones. While the trade press may have a lot more detail about a specific sector than say the business pages of a national daily newspaper, it tends to be rather conservative. Many of these journals are written by a very few people. They rely on company briefings and press releases to provide the bulk of their content, a lot of which is reproduced unaltered. They may be quite close to key people working in their sector. They are probably reliant on income from advertising by leading companies in that sector. They are very unlikely therefore to be provocative, critical or controversial. You need to take account of this.

- Advocacy sites – These are very obviously partisan, and generally run by pressure groups, political parties and other non-governmental organizations (NGOs), or sometimes by aggrieved customers or shareholder action groups. They can be very helpful in providing the 'unofficial view', but they may reflect only the opinion of a tiny minority, or even just one person. They need to be assessed against other sources of information.

- Business and marketing pages – Although company websites may contain useful information, such as details of their latest annual report, their purpose is to promote the company and its products. They will present the best picture that they can of themselves and should therefore be regarded with the deepest scepticism. Although it might be interesting to know what a company officially thinks about itself, you should never rely on company websites as a main source of information.

- **Personal web pages** – You need to think about why they are there. They tend to be produced by the mad, the sad and the obsessive, but yet again they may have some insight into an aspect of a business or product that you had not thought about.

- **Entertainment sites** – the sole purpose of these sites is to entertain you and to market something. They are highly unlikely to be helpful in gathering secondary data unless your dissertation is on something like Internet shopping.

(Developed from O' Dochartaigh (2003) *The Internet Research Handbook*.)

How Do I Know that I am Looking in the Right Place?

This is necessarily a very difficult question to answer, as it depends very much on the topic of the dissertation or assignment you are working on. Our suggestion is that once you are sure that you have exhausted the resources of your university or college library and any other academic libraries to which you have access, as well as the dedicated academic online databases, you should then work through the hierarchy of Internet resources we have suggested above. You could start with a very simple search using Google. Type in your search term or terms and eliminate from the results immediately any sites that do not end with the domain name .edu or .ac (followed, except for US sites, by the country name) or that are not from an obvious academic source. For example, the following are university websites:

- **www.brookes.ac.uk – Oxford Brookes University;**

- **www.anu.edu.au – Australian National University;**

- **www.cbs.dk – Copenhagen Business School;**

- **www.sbm.temple.edu – Fox School of Business and Management, Temple University, USA.**

Many university and college course guides talk about demonstrating that you have used a 'wide range' of sources, or a 'breadth' of sources. But they seldom tell you what they mean by breadth or how wide the range of sources is supposed to be. In the context of collecting secondary data, a wide range must be one that from your point of view demonstrates that you have looked in lots of different places and considered using many different types of information. Reference lists in dissertations should not be one long list of websites for example, or a long list of textbooks and second-hand data. If you are using government statistics, for example, go back to the original source, which is usually the national statistics office of the relevant country or international organization, and is generally freely available on the Internet and often in English. Do not use statistics that have been reproduced in textbooks. They may be inaccurate and out of date.

In thinking about the main sources of secondary information in business and management, it may be helpful to think that there are six broad categories of sources of data. You should strive to make sure you have demonstrated that you have accessed information that falls into each of these categories. This will help you to meet the requirement to show breadth of knowledge and access to a wide range of sources.

The six categories are:

- **media sources – print newspapers and magazines such as the *Economist*, television programmes and online news services;**

- **practitioner sources – the trade press, professional journals, and publications by professional groups and bodies;**

- **government sources – national and international government statistics and those from bodies such as the United Nations (UN) and EU, World Bank and IMF; policy documents, laws, regulations, parliamentary debates and committee reports;**

- **commercial sources – published market studies commissioned for a specific purpose or audience such as stockbroker reports and published market research;**

- **company sources – internal records, annual reports and financial statements, press releases and company websites;**

- **academic sources – books and journal articles written by academics working in the further and higher education sectors.**

When Can I Stop?

It can be very difficult to work out if you have got enough information. A typical Masters' dissertation – if there is such a thing – would probably include well over a hundred references to different sources, and may have many more. DMS projects may have slightly fewer references to literature, but may have more practitioner-based sources, but they still have to demonstrate a thorough grounding in theory (see Chapter 1). A simple answer would be that you could stop when you have sufficient information to answer your research objectives and questions, but it is not easy to tell that in advance of writing up your dissertation. One clue to when you are getting near the end is if authors that you have already read or documents that you have already consulted keep turning up again and again, or if you start to read articles where you have already seen yourself the majority of the references cited. Check with the list above that you have actually covered a sufficient variety of sources. Your supervisors will encourage you to write an early draft of the whole dissertation or parts of it and their comments on this will help you to identify significant gaps and holes in your sources. The very act of drafting a chapter or two and actually sitting down to write can show you that you are relying on too few sources for the bulk of your information and indicate where significant gaps are. Occasionally, important secondary sources will be published while you are writing or just about to finish your dissertation; if this is the case and a new important text or article appears you should try to include it in your work in order to show that you are up to date with the subject. Months will pass while you collect sources of information and conduct research and then write it up and you do not want to be caught out by your examiners, who will feel that you *should* be up to date at Masters' level.

Once you have established a framework for analysing your data (see Chapter 7) and have started writing it up, you can always start collecting further information in a much more narrowly defined area. This can make later searching more purposeful and fruitful.

Practical Worked Example

Researching Sustainable Consumption

If you were interested in researching the growth of sustainable consumption and its impact on business strategy as a dissertation topic, you should start by going to your university's library. A good place to start would be the reference section where you might find UN, OECD, EU and national data about trends in gross national product (GNP) and consumption. You could also find published market research reports that relate to countries' consumption patterns. National governments and NGOs (such as charities, pressure groups and international organizations) will have published reports on sustainability and the environment and these would be another good source of information – their websites should contain links to many of their publications. Company reports would be useful to browse through if you wanted to see how individual organizations and sectors were responding to sustainable consumption.

Having gathered a lot of information from the reference section, you could then move on to academic journals. Journals such as the *Journal of Business Ethics* or the leading environmental journals such as *Business Strategy and the Environment*, and leading consumer journals such as *International Journal of Consumer Studies* would be a useful source of relevant articles whose references you could then follow up. Textbooks might add to your body of knowledge in this area; for example, there are a number about business strategies for the environment and others on related issues such as green marketing. You would by now have enough material from a variety of different paper-based sources to read further on this topic. You will then have to make some decisions about the relative merits of some of the material you have collected.

Summary

This chapter has focused on how to assess the sources that you use to collect material for your research. It has offered a practical distinction between the material that should be included in a literature review and useful material that can be included elsewhere in you dissertation. Sources of information have been categorized to assist you in gathering a wide range of material. The chapter has outlined the issues surrounding information from the Internet and the need to be critical in evaluating the usefulness of information derived from this source. The core aim of the chapter was to communicate the need for rigour in your information collection.

Suggested Activity

Use the checklist below to evaluate a document you have found on the Internet. For each question, write down whether the answer you have given is positive or negative. Add up the score at the end – the higher the positive score the greater the weight you should be able to give the document.

Checklist: Evaluating a World Wide Web Document

✓ Is it clear *who* is responsible for the document? [Who is the author; what is the organization; is there a publisher; a copyright statement might tell you this.]

✓ Is there any information about the person or organization responsible for the document? [This might help you to judge how authoritative or reputable it is.]

✓ Is there a printed version? [This might reinforce its authority.]

✓ Are the sources used in the document clearly listed? [This should add to their credibility and make it possible to verify them.]

✓ Is there an editor, or has it been through an editorial process? [It should be possible to tell – for example, the document might tell you who edited it and it should add credibility, and might improve the accuracy.

✓ Is the grammar and spelling correct? [This should add credibility, but many documents in English on the web have been written or translated by non-native speakers and incorrect grammar unfortunately does not necessarily mean they are fake.]

✓ Are the affiliations and biases of the author clearly stated?

✓ Is any advertising clearly distinguished from information? [As it has to be, for example, in British newspapers. Be doubly wary if a seemingly impartial document ends up by trying to sell you something. Marketing claims on the Internet are not regulated by anyone.]

✓ Is there a publication date on the printed version of the web document?

✓ Alternatively, are there dates for when the document was first produced or first put on the web?

✓ Are there dates for when the document was last updated or revised? [There are lots of very out of date documents on the web now.]

(Adapted from O' Dochartaigh, 2003)

Hint: the more negative answers, the lower the credibility and authority of this particular document

Discussion Questions

1   Why is it important to show that you have used a wide range of sources?

2   Look through the secondary information you have started to collect. Can you defend your selection?

3   How can a Masters' student demonstrate 'rigour' in selecting sources of secondary data?

Further Reading

O' Dochartaigh, N. (2003) *The Internet Research Handbook.* **London: Sage.** An intelligent and helpful text which provides much needed advice on the quality of Internet resources.

6 How to Read Critically

How Do I Evaluate What I Have Read?

The aim of this chapter is to show you how to become a critical reader of typical academic literature in business and management, and to emphasize that this is a key requirement of postgraduate education. Although the focus is on developing your skills at reading academic journal articles, the same principles and approaches can be applied to all your academic reading.

How Do You Spot Academic Journal Articles and Why Should You Read Them?

Students even at Masters' level have often asked us why we put so much emphasis on the need to read academic journal articles, rather than rely on summaries of their content that are conveyed through textbooks and occasionally the business press. They point out that it is very rare to come across managers who spend their leisure time reading the *British Journal of Management*, for example, though they might well read the *Financial Times* or the business pages of major newspapers. Reading academic journal articles is vital whether you are pursuing a practitioner-focused MBA or a more theoretical MSc, and it is perhaps worth it at this stage to list the main reasons:

1   **The appropriate use of journal articles demonstrates to the reader and the examiner the depth and breadth of your knowledge on a subject.**

2   **Your references to academic journals can demonstrate how up to date you are in your awareness of the developments in your chosen subject.**

3   **Textbooks can never be up to date and tend to reflect yesterday's thinking. Relying on textbooks that are often developed from older journal articles may mean that your work is dated.**

4   **Academic journal articles tend to look towards the future and may even suggest areas that you could explore in your own research (see Chapter 3).**

5 The requirement at Masters' level to 'synthesize' theory and practice indicates a need to know about the theory, which can be found in journal articles.

6 The inclusion of a range of journal articles and references to them is usually a mandatory marking criterion.

It may sound odd, but one question that university teachers never seem to answer is what exactly *is* an academic journal article? This can be particularly confusing for business and management students, as many university libraries contain a mixture of academic journals and much more practically focused literature, as do lots of the online databases. There is also an amazing and bewildering variety of journal titles. You simply can't tell what exactly you are going to get from the title – *Hardware Trades Journal* is not an academic journal and nor is *Marketing*, but the *Journal of Marketing* certainly is. So how do you spot them when you are new to the subject area?

One simple approach is to look at the structure of the articles. Academic journal articles tend to be long compared to magazine articles – 5000 words or more – they carry lots of references (mostly to other journal articles) and tend not to have any illustrations, though they have many charts and tables. They do not normally carry paid-for advertising. But the *Harvard Business Review*, an example of a very prestigious journal in which to have an article published, breaks at least two of these rules (lacks references and includes illustrations). The key distinction is really that an academic journal article goes through a critical peer review process before it is published. If you are in any doubt about the status of an academic journal, look at the 'note for contributors' section (usually at the back of each volume, sometimes inside the front cover). This can also be found on the main menu page of the journal publisher's website. Here is a quotation from one well-known journal's guidelines on manuscript submission:

> *Management Learning* publishes theoretical and research based papers which are usually 5–7000 words. We do recognise that some work may call for shorter or longer expression. All submissions should incorporate critique and consider the learning implications of the work and ideas described. An editor will review each paper and if judged as incorporating the characteristics above and covering material suitable to the aims of the Journal, will be sent to two reviewers for blind review. The decision will be made as to whether the paper be accepted as is, invited for further revision and review, or rejected based on the reviewers' recommendations. (See www.sagepub.com/journalManuscript.aspx?pid=207&sc=1)

The key words here are that the paper will go through a process of peer review involving two 'blind' referees, who will not be told the name of the author. And the author will never be told the name of the reviewers. When the editor receives the manuscript he or she will decide whether to reject it outright or to send it out without the author's name on it to two reviewers who are experts in the field. They will be asked to comment on it anonymously. These comments are then fed back to the author, who may be asked to revise the paper, taking the comments into account, or the paper may be rejected altogether. After the author has revised the paper, it may be re-reviewed by the original reviewers or even by one or two others, before the editor finally accepts it for publication.

This peer review process is a guarantee of academic acceptability, but it does not mean that the article is necessarily brilliantly researched, or well written, let alone that it is up to date. The process of peer review has been criticized for enforcing conformity and helping to confirm the status quo, so that research using unorthodox methods or that challenges assumptions tends to stay unpublished. It is difficult to find hard evidence of this. One thing is certain – it does slow the publication process up. The whole process of review can take at least 2 years or more from when the article was finished, so the research you are reading about may have been carried out several years before you first see it written up.

How to Start Reading an Academic Journal Article: What to Look For

Once you have identified your academic journal articles you need to develop a system for reading them. We have carried out research with groups of students and staff (see Smallbone and Quinton, 2004) to see if there is a good way of doing this. Many people suggest it is important to first read the title and the abstract, though not all articles have an abstract and the abstract is not always helpful. If there is no abstract, the article may contain a summary, which can be more useful.

Sometimes words in the title written after a colon give a clue as to what it is really about, while the first few words are really written to catch your eye and may not tell you very much. For example, an article by Robin Wensley in *Business Strategy Review* has the title 'Explaining Success' before the colon, which could apply to virtually anything. When you read further you realize that it is about market share and its relationship to profitability and builds on earlier articles: 'the rule of ten percent and the example of market share' (Wensley, 1997).

Some readers go to the back of the academic article after they have read the title and abstract. They are checking the references. This is only really worth doing if you know what you are checking them for. Sometimes it may be length and number – though it is difficult to say that the more published works the author references, the better the article. If only it were that simple! It may be that the article is so original that little has been written on the subject before. If there are a lot of references and the article is on a subject that is relevant to your work, you have the opportunity to follow up some of the references to extend your reading, as well as to draw on what the author has used from these sources.

Authors who reference mainly themselves might be marked down on grounds of vanity and shameless self-promotion. They might still be worth reading, but you could ask yourself whether, if they mainly read their own work, they will be able to offer the reader a good grasp of varying opinions and research in their particular field. Another reason for checking the references at some stage is to see if the works the authors are relying on and referencing have much academic status. This is very difficult for students new to the subject to judge, but one rule of thumb is to ask your teachers or supervisor for a list of the top six (most highly-rated) journals in your particular field. All academic journals are ranked for prestige and academic excellence in a number of league tables, with the top-most rated the hardest for academic authors to get their work into. It is well worth finding out which ones are the best in your sub-field of marketing or organizational behaviour, for example. Do be aware that experts in these subjects will also try to get their work published in the top general management journals as well, so you should also always consider these.

Even if the article you are reading is not from one of the top-ranked journals, it may still be well worth reading, but it might be worth checking if the references include at least some work that has been published in journals that are in the top rank. An additional complication for business and management students is that business academics frequently draw on sources from other academic disciplines. Their work may include references to articles in psychology, sociology and economics journals. This is what makes the subject so interesting, so do not despair; you cannot be expected to know how rigorous these sources are as well. You will probably find that you do not need to follow all these up, unless it is an area of particular focus for you, such as in writing your dissertation, where you may in any case be forced to look in non-business subject areas in order to find sufficient sources (see Chapter 5).

Once you have read the title, the abstract and checked out the references, there are still a few other criteria that can help you decide immediately whether the article is worth reading. When was the article written and when was the research it reports on actually done? If the article is wholly theoretical, how recent are the references – does it reflect up-to-date thinking? Another interesting question is, why was the research undertaken? Does the author state near the beginning his or her rationale or justification for carrying out this piece of research and for writing the article? Perhaps it forms part of a bigger research project?

In business and management, 'currency' is key. The business environment is constantly changing and academics quite often struggle to keep abreast of current practice and thinking. It is therefore important that the issues reported on in academic journal articles are up to date and have not been superseded by later research and thinking, which may have been published in other journals. Of course there are some 'classic' journal articles and your teachers may well direct you to read those as well.

A further issue to think about is the standing of the author, or authors, of the article and what were the data collection methods. The journal article should tell you where the authors work, and their job titles, but it is difficult when it is a subject that is unfamiliar to you to guess the quality of the article from this information. If one of the authors is from your university or college, then it is probably a good idea to read it in any case. If the author has used primary research, the methods or methodology section should tell you about their data collection methods. Read carefully to find out the sample size – if it was a quantitative study – and the way the sample was recruited, the checks that were used to assure data quality and where the research was carried out. If, for example, the study was very small-scale, it might be interesting because you might want to repeat it, but it might also be limited in what you can generalize from it. See Chapter 9 for more on how to assess the validity and reliability of the data, and for a discussion of some of the rather controversial issues that surround questions of generalization.

Asking Questions

Once you have checked the date of the article, when the research was done, and as far as you can the author's credentials, and skim-read the whole article, you are ready to ask yourself a few more questions about it. Using questions as prompts is an excellent method of digging beneath the surface of what you read. Socrates believed that we all have latent ability in this area and that through practice individuals could develop a rigorous approach to identifying, examining and then solving their own challenges. As researchers and managers this is an essential skill that should help you in all aspects of life, including making decisions.

Later in this chapter we have included two frameworks for analysing and critically reading academic journal articles from business and management, although they can be used in other subject areas as well. We hope that you will find them useful in your reading. We use them ourselves and encourage our students to use them in coursework assignments and when reading for their dissertations. They have been developed by us with our students, drawing on a number of other authors who also present critical reading frameworks, which we have included in our Further Reading section at the end of the chapter. We have developed them from reading the teaching literature about academic reading and from holding reading workshops with our students where we have tried to analyse a range of different journal articles about business and management. The frameworks are designed to prompt you into thinking more deeply about the content and the message of the articles you are reading to enable you to adopt a critical approach to your reading. There are two frameworks that you can use. One is designed to be used with academic journal articles that are based around reporting on some primary research, which is usually aimed at testing or constructing a theory. The other is for those journal articles that are wholly theoretical. These might be in the form of a literature review or research agenda, or might be developing a conceptual theory that is not actually tested in the article.

General questions that you may wish to ask of any academic study that uses primary data, regardless of the methods used, include:

1   **What is the rationale for this article?**

2   **What is the stated purpose of the article?**

3   **What were the methods or procedures used and were they appropriate to the purpose?**

4   **Does the discussion/interpretation make sense?**

5   **Is the conclusion justified?**

These questions can be asked of both quantitative and qualitative research projects that have employed very different methods. For example, a research project about consumers' perceptions of air travel that uses narrative as the central data collection method, or a project focusing on an organization's stock price movements before and after an acquisition that uses statistical tests as the main method can both be critically questioned by using the question prompts above (Girden, 1996).

In the next section we discuss the reading frameworks (shown in Figure 6.1) and provide further explanations of how to use them to help you read critically. The subheadings are the ones we have used in these frameworks.

Using the Critical Reading Frameworks: What to Look At

At an early stage in reading an article, it is important to understand the author's perspective and approach. If primary data is being collected, was the approach inductive or deductive? Can you work out the author's view of how knowledge is constructed (his or her 'ontology' – see Chapter 1)? This can provide vital clues to how and why the article has been written in the way it has. The answers to these questions will provide

Framework for deconstructing journal articles using primary data

What to look at	
Date – when was the research reported on actually done?	
How current are the results?	
What are the author's credentials?	
Is the approach inductive or deductive?	
Data collection methods: what did they actually do?	
In what ways is this article similar to or different from others you might have read?	
Style	
Is the article constructed clearly?	
Can you follow the argument through a logical development?	
Does the use of tables, diagrams, and charts add value to the conclusions or the explanation?	
Analysis	
What is the central issue dealt with in the paper?	
Is there a particular cultural bias?	
What assumptions have been made, e.g. about the generalizability of the results?	
What is the evidence supporting these assumptions?	
Reflection	
How do you respond to what the author is saying?	
How do you rate this article?	
How does it relate to other concepts you have come across?	
How can you verify the results?	
Does it point to further research in a particular direction?	
Is it relevant to your current work?	

Framework for deconstructing journal articles using theory

What to look at	
Date – when was it written, revised, published?	
How current is the discussion?	
What are the author's credentials?	
What is the author's perspective? Where is he or she coming from?	
In what ways is this article similar to or different from others you might have read?	
Style	
Is the article constructed clearly?	
Can you follow the argument through a logical development?	
Does the use of tables, diagrams and charts add value to the conclusions or the explanation?	
Analysis	
What is the central issue dealt with in the paper?	
What assumptions have been made? Are they *explicit*, if so what are they? Are they *implicit*, if so what are they?	
Are the sources drawn from a variety of areas?	
Are the sources drawn from a wide range of different authors?	
Is there an apparent cultural bias?	
Reflection	
How do you respond to what the author is saying?	
How do you rate this article?	
If this article is purely theoretical, how do you assess its academic quality?	
How does it relate to other concepts you have come across?	
Does it point to further research in a particular direction?	
Is it relevant to your current work?	

Figure 6.1   Reading frameworks

you with a very useful source of comment when you are writing your assignment, particularly if you are writing a literature review.

If the research has involved the collection of primary data, you should think about which methods were used and whether there is evidence to support the use of those methods. For example, if questionnaires and observation were used as data collection tools, are there references to other occurrences of using such techniques? (See Chapter 9 about the reliability of your research.)

The number and type of sample size or respondents or participants used in the research also needs questioning. It is surprising how many published academic articles have relied on students as their sample without mentioning the problems this can create. Are students representative of anything other than the student population? Can you spot gaps or flaws in the method as written up? Often in academic papers, the method section is the one that is cut down in terms of the number of words to fulfil the word limit. This editing makes reading and thinking critically about the method more difficult.

Continuing down the framework headings, the next question to consider is how similar or different this article is from others that you might have read on the same subject? Again the answer to this will be very helpful when you are writing it up, as you can group similar articles together when you are discussing them, or compare and contrast dissimilar articles to highlight points that you wish to make.

Style

Although you do not need to comment on an author's literary style, you will need to understand and critique the author's use of argument and the style of the article can be either a help or a hindrance in working out what this is. If the article has not been constructed clearly and you cannot follow the argument through a logical development, it may be that the author is muddled or unclear in his or her thinking, which could be a fundamental flaw. The content of the argument presented in the article will need to be analysed (see below), but at this stage it is important to be satisfied that there is a coherent argument that develops logically so that the reader can follow it.

Many academic articles contain tables, diagrams, and charts to illustrate or develop the concepts they also describe in words. These may or may not be helpful. The temptation is to simply copy them (with a reference to the original) into your notes or straight into your assignment or dissertation. But, in our experience, these charts and diagrams do not always really add value to the words. Do not be afraid to pull diagrams apart. What do they really show? Why are the arrows pointing in a particular direction, for example? What would happen if you reversed them? Do the labels on the boxes make sense? Does the diagram tell you something new or really explain what the author is saying? Proposed models and working models and diagrams are just that, so although a critique of them may be useful, it is worth remembering that the models may still be in development (though this should be made clear by the author).

It may be that you have the sort of brain that can visualize the theory being discussed much better if it is depicted in a diagram than as words or in addition to words on paper. You have a strongly visual intelligence. You may want to turn the words in the paper into your own diagram. For example, you can use the mapping techniques described in Chapter 3 to plot the argument being put forward by the authors of the article.

Analysis

You should by now have a reasonable idea about what is the central issue that the paper deals with. It is not always crystal clear – some academics seem to delight in being obscure, so you might have to dig a bit to find it. Occasionally the focus highlighted in the abstract or the central issue as given in the introduction is not the one dealt with in the main body of the paper. In these instances, the author has gone off at a tangent and researched something other than the stated central issue, which can be very frustrating for the reader. You can only find this out by reading the paper and paying particular attention to the objectives, method (if given) and the subsequent discussion.

Once you have worked out the central issue, you can start to analyse the argument used in the paper. By 'argument', we do not mean a quarrel or even the formal logic of the article. What is meant here is the way in which the author presents his or her conclusions and how this is justified by supporting evidence. So what you are trying to analyse is the author's theoretical standpoint (where is he or she coming from on this?), the quality of any evidence he or she produces to back it up, how he or she links it to theory, and evaluates it in the text and diagrams of the article. There are a variety of approaches that you can adopt when analysing an argument. One author suggests 11 different ways of critiquing an article based on different philosophical perspectives with the 11th an attempt to combine the previous ten (Metcalfe, 2003). Our approach is simpler: we are trying to help you make sure that you understand the articles that you read and that you can use them in an appropriate way in your written work.

It is important to identify the author's assumptions in any journal article. They may be explicitly stated, but there may be additional ones, and they may all be hidden or implicit. If the assumptions are explicit, can you identify any evidence or references to other authors that might give support to those assumptions? You can ask additional 'what' questions that may help to dig some of the implicit assumptions out. The author may be addressing a particular issue or theme in the prevalent literature on his or her subject, and should be able to justify why it is necessary to tackle it as an issue and its importance for scholarship in this subject. The author may be addressing a particular audience, for example, from one particular culture, profession or social group, and this may have strongly affected the underlying assumptions and the way he or she presents his or her argument. Another assumption might be that the author assumes that you share his or her views that a particular explanation is appropriate, or that words should be interpreted in one particular way.

For articles based on primary data collection, it is interesting to examine the author's assumptions about the extent to which the findings can be generalized to other populations, countries, social groups and cultures, and to unpick the evidence that supports these kinds of generalizations. For example, the study may have been conducted among suburban households in one area of the USA. It may not be possible to generalize to other similar suburbs in the USA because of regional variations in culture and lifestyle, let alone to other countries and foreign cultures. You need to assess the author's views on this and if they are not stated you may need to look carefully to identify the implicit assumptions.

For articles that are wholly theoretical, it is very important to examine carefully the range, variety and depth of the sources that are used and are referenced. Have you come across any of the authors used? Are they recognized authorities in the field? A quick search of the author's name, if it is at all unusual, on Google will give you a good idea of how many papers he or she has written, where he or she is based and his or her probable academic standing, if you do not know already. On some academic databases you can click on the references, and they will take you to the article referred to or to other work by the author, but this can be a haphazard process.

Cultural bias is an interesting issue because it can be difficult to spot, especially if you happen to be from the prevalent culture. But it is very important to recognize that a lot of research and writing in management and business is very bound to one culture. In looking at references, you may even find that the sources used come from just a few journals and these in themselves may reflect one particular culture or way of looking at knowledge. For example, a number of French and American management journals are very heavily biased towards quantitative methods and a strongly positivist view of research and reality.

Reflection

Critical reading is not just about trying to pull an article apart so that its bones and its strong and weak points are revealed, you have to think and learn to reflect on what you have read. At a deeper level, you might also like to start reflecting on the process of reflection – how have you approached your reading and reflection and what assumptions did you make, for example? It might be a requirement of your course that you incorporate an element of reflection into your academic work and this may be assessed separately. Reflection on reading can form part of this. See Chapter 8 for more on this.

The process of reflecting on reading seems to generate a lot of 'why' questions. Adopting this questioning approach can help to force you to confront and explore issues at a rather deeper level than the 'what' questions suggested earlier. It is very helpful to record your response to the 'message' of the authors of the articles you have been reading, as it will enable you to form a judgement about the merits of the article and the arguments it contains. You can ask yourself, is the article convincing, at least in part? Has it prompted some further thoughts in your mind and, if so, what are they? Is it irritating and, if so, why? Does it make you feel uncomfortable? Again you need to probe why this is the case. Perhaps it is prompting you to take action – such as to carry out your own research project in order to verify the findings. Are the findings verifiable in any case? If not, why are they not? Is this a weakness? Sometimes it can be helpful to make a judgement on the whole article and to score it out of ten, or to rate it on a number of criteria such as relevance, novelty, links to other research, depth and so on. You can create your own list of criteria and scoring system and even build up a bank of scored articles. This may be very helpful when deciding what to include in your literature review.

Linking articles together in your mind is a crucial part of being able to write a decent literature review, and it can be helpful to kick start this process by recording how the article you are reading relates to other reading and concepts you have come across. The links between articles may be surprising – there are obvious ones where, for example, authors are testing out the same propositions in different conditions, or following similar methodologies, but sometimes articles on different themes or topics may still provide interesting links to each other that you can then explore or develop further.

The best articles may be worth reading for themselves but they may not be relevant to your current work. You need to make a quick judgement about this, but do keep everything you read until you are really convinced that you will not use it. In writing up your assignment or dissertation, you may well find that the process of writing takes you down paths that turn out to be worth including after all and you can then return to your unused notes for inspiration. In any event, use the frameworks below to help to capture your thoughts because as you read further, more thoughts will be stimulated, and it is so easy to lose the previous ones.

We have chosen four academic journal articles of the types you may very well come across in your literature search. These include two with an international focus (one by Miyauchi and Perry (1999) on marketing fresh fruit to Japanese consumers and exploring the issues for Australian exporters, and one by Shoham and Dalakas (2003) on family consumer decision-making in Israel and the role of teens and parents). We have also used one that creates a model (Raju (1995) on consumer behaviour in global markets and its application to Eastern Europe and the Third World) and one that adopts a strongly qualitative approach (Bayley and Nancarrow, (1998) on a qualitative exploration of the phenomenon of impulse purchasing). By taking small sections from each of these papers, we will demonstrate how you might be able to take apart an academic journal article and use the frameworks provided earlier in the chapter to help you create a critical literature review. This is just an illustrative example and when using a framework to analyse a single article you would obviously want to go into greater depth.

Practical Worked Example

Actual Journal Articles

Framework for deconstructing journal articles using primary data

What to look at	
Date – when was it written, revised, published?	For example, Miyauchi and Perry's article on exporting fruit from Australia to Japan was published in 1999, but submitted for review in September 1996 and uses secondary data from 1985 and 1993. Therefore this information may be out of date.
How current are the results?	In the example above, not very.
Author's credentials?	In the Shoham and Dalakas (2003) article, we can see that both are academics at universities in the two countries covered by the article; they are relatively junior.
Is the approach inductive or deductive?	The approach taken by Bayley and Nancarrow (1998) is wholly inductive and appropriate for the type of research undertaken and the journal published in, but the results are exploratory.
Data collection methods: what did they actually do?	Friendship pair interviews and self-scripts were employed by Bayley and Nancarrow (1998) using three researchers to cross-check and act as controls.
In what ways is this article similar or different from others you might have read?	It (Bayley and Nancarrow, 1998) is different, as it uses unusual data collection tools, but it is similar to other studies in taking an inductive approach to look at consumer behaviour.
Style	
Is it constructed clearly?	The (Bayley and Nancarrow, 1998) article is disjointed with the objectives placed late on in the paper, and a messy layout with numerous different subsections, which makes it less cohesive.

example continues

example continues

Can you follow the argument through a logical development?	The Bayley and Nancarrow article requires several read-throughs to untangle the logical argument.
Does the use of tables, diagrams and charts add value to the conclusions or the explanation?	The Raju paper proposes to create a model that offers a general framework to understand consumer behaviour in any global market. However, the model itself is little more than a checklist and certainly not a paradigm.
Analysis	
What is the central issue dealt with in the paper?	Miyauchi and Perry clearly identify their focus, which is a case study of export marketing of fresh produce.
What assumptions have been made? Are they *explicit*, if so what are they? Are they *implicit*, if so what are they?	The Shoham and Dalakas article is founded upon the earlier work of Hofstede, but no explicit critique is given to the limitations of Hofstede's work on cultural dimensions. The implicit assumption therefore is that this earlier work is valid and reliable.
What is the evidence supporting these assumptions?	There is none (Shoham and Dalakas).
Are the sources drawn from a variety of areas?	Raju's paper uses some academic articles and is supported by numerous examples taken from American business magazines. The sources should have been expanded.
Are they drawn from a wide range of different authors?	The sources used by Miyauchi and Perry are very limited and thus the paper is constrained in its discussion.
Is there an apparent cultural bias?	In the Shoham and Dalakas article, there is a heavy reliance on American empirical studies that may not be appropriate in an Israeli research context.
Reflection	
How do you respond to what the author is saying?	The Bayley and Nancarrow paper was interesting to read, depite the irritation of too many vignettes as examples.

How do you rate this article?	Miyauchi and Perry's findings are tentative and need confirmation, possibly through secondary information and also further primary data collection.
How does it relate to other concepts you have come across?	Miyauchi and Perry look at a market and a product where little information was available, but it does relate to concepts such as market segmentation and market entry strategies.
How can you verify the results?	Must re-examine secondary data and collect more (Miyauchi and Perry).
Does it point to further research in a particular direction?	The Raju paper offers a long list of ideas that could be developed further in future research.
Is it relevant to your current work?	Possibly.

Summary

This chapter has focused on the practical aspect of how to read critically as this is an essential skill for Masters' level students. Questions that you should ask yourself when reading a journal article have been proposed, such as 'what is the purpose of this piece of research'? Two frameworks have been included to assist in deconstructing the two main types of article, those based upon theory and those involving primary research.

Suggested Activity

Choose a journal article that you need to read for an assignment or for your dissertation. Skim-read it and then use one of the frameworks given earlier to analyse it further. Use the note-taking framework suggested in Chapter 2 to record what information you need from the article. Clip the two pieces together and file carefully.

Discussion Questions

1 Do you think there is too much emphasis placed on reading academic journal articles for management research? If so, why?

2 What are the advantages and disadvantages of deconstructing academic journal articles?

Further Reading

Blaxter, L., Hughes, C. and Tight, M. (2001) *How to Research*. **Buckingham: Open University Press.** A rather basic text, but contains many useful hints and advice. Chapter 4 is on reading for research.

November, P. (2002) 'Teaching marketing theory: A hermeneutic approach', *Marketing Theory,* **2(1): 114–32.** An interesting discussion of how a university teacher encouraged his students to tackle some key academic journal articles and the approach he adopted.

7 Organizing and Analysing What You Have Read and Researched

How Do I Sort Out My Information?

Many students have difficulty in structuring their collected thoughts and material. The aim of this chapter is to enable you to make the most of all the data that you have collected whether while carrying out your primary or your secondary research. This chapter will not address the various data analysis tools and techniques that you can use, as there are numerous textbooks on data analysis that cover this area well. Rather, this chapter offers advice on how to collate, sort and appraise all the material you have collected, so that you can commence the process of analysis.

When Should I Stop Collecting Data and Start Analysing It?

Many researchers ask, 'how much data is enough'? There is no absolute answer to this frequently asked question. The 'how much' depends on the nature of your chosen topic and factors such as whether you are exploring a concept or trying to test a theory. You do need to make sure that you keep up to date with newly published editions of academic journals, just in case something new on your subject is about to come out. Similarly, if your sources of industry or company data start to repeat the same information and to reiterate the same views or statistics, you may well have enough to start your analysis.

It can be very difficult to work out if you have got enough information. A typical Masters' dissertation – if there is such a thing – would probably include well over a hundred references to different sources, and may have many more. DMS projects may have slightly fewer references to literature, but may have more practitioner-based sources, but they still have to demonstrate a thorough grounding in theory (see Chapter 1). A simple answer would be that you could stop when you have sufficient information to answer your research objectives and questions, but it is not easy to tell that in advance of writing up your dissertation.

If you are collecting primary data in a qualitative study and your respondents or participants appear to reinforce each other, perhaps by using the same vocabulary to describe a situation, you may have collected enough raw data. In some studies, you can gain as great an insight into a management situation by conducting six interviews as 36 and by using content analysis to unravel what was said and why. If you have reached your given target for the sample size of your quantitative study – with your questionnaire, for example, as outlined in your research design – you can then stop collecting raw data. The quantity of data you collect will also be influenced by how you intend to analyse it. Performing statistical tests on data collected from a sample size of 25 respondents will give meaningless results, whereas the same tests performed on data from a sample of 475 should provide you with useful results. So you need always to consider your purpose and research objectives, that is, what you actually set out to discover, as well as the data collection tools you used and your chosen analysis methods when you are deciding how much data is enough. See Chapter 5, 'When can I stop' (page 77), for advice on deciding whether you have collected enough data.

Dealing with the Secondary Data You Collect

Students and researchers frequently feel daunted by the sheer amount of material that they collect in the course of one research project. Inevitably, some of the material you have collected will not be included in the final, completed dissertation. Unfortunately, collecting more than you need is part of the research process and as you progress in your data collection, you will narrow down your searches as your focus narrows, with the inevitable result that some material you collected early on will be discarded. Don't be disheartened by thinking you have wasted valuable time collecting information and then not using it. The actual process of collecting the material will have helped to develop your thinking about the subject anyway. Knowing what to leave out is an indication that you have learnt what the key areas are that have to be included and an important indicator of the increase in your expertise in the subject area.

Filtering and categorizing

Business dissertations involve the collection of vast amounts of material, and you need to organize it so that you can maximize its usefulness. You need to find a systematic way of both sorting and summarizing the data you have collected, and you may find you need to devise a method of coding your data before you can analyse it properly. An initial filtering process may help to clarify what your purpose is. Try to sort information into levels of importance (interesting but limited, relevant but not vital, vital, and so on) just to help with your own focus before you go any further. You may repeat the filtering phase several times and bits of information might get promoted or demoted at subsequent sessions.

Following the initial filter, you should try and begin the process of grouping your secondary data into categories. These categories should help by adding understanding and depth to your research questions or objectives. Categorizing your secondary data should create order out of chaos and will then make the subsequent analysis less time consuming and more pertinent to realizing your objectives. The initial categories you choose are important, but they can always be changed later on. You may well find that you have collected your secondary data chronologically, as you tracked back through issues of journals to chart the evolution of a theory, perhaps, or trawled backwards through company reports and websites. Collecting your data in this way makes a lot of sense – it enables you to make sure, for instance, that you have not left out a particular year in the company results, but it will be of little use for you when writing up your dissertation. You now need to re-categorize it.

You may want to categorize your secondary data by business sector, or an academic theme, or possibly by the research methodology employed that you are considering using in your own project. For example, if you were thinking of using structured observation, you might find it very useful to keep descriptions of the use of this research method when you come across it in your reading. Other categories you might create could be the type of source, the research question it raises, or the research question it answers. The categories used should be discrete and exclusive, if possible. You will want to avoid the problem of 'where should I put this piece of paper, as it belongs to many groups'? Unfortunately, this is not always easy and you may well need to introduce a system of cross-referencing. This can also be helpful later on when you want to link your categories and show how they are interconnected. Drawing a learning map of the linkages and keeping a copy in front of each file or folder where you keep your assemblage of papers may prove invaluable later on. Another way to show links is to use coloured stickers or to write on different coloured paper or in different coloured pen when you want to show that something belongs in more than one place. Students frequently find themselves with piles of papers loosely sorted into draft categories at this stage; do not feel overwhelmed if this is you.

Because at some stage in your dissertation you should demonstrate that you have drawn on a wide range of different data sources (see Chapter 5), an obvious means of grouping your secondary data might seem to be by the type of source. However, that will really only help you to write a couple of paragraphs of your final dissertation where you discuss the types of sources you used and their limitations. If you think it would be helpful later on, you could sort your secondary data into types of source and then write a draft of these paragraphs, before re-categorizing your data into themes that are more helpful for the rest of your dissertation. Establishing categories can take time, but once you have decided on the categories, you should stick to them. It can be really helpful to write them up on a piece of flip chart paper and stick that on a wall, or on a white board if you have access to one. You can then come back to them and amend them slightly as and when you need to and relate them, where necessary, to academic themes or your research objectives.

Classification of your material is not about making judgements as to the value of each piece you have collected, but it is about sorting material and documents to make the process of analysis rigorous but more straightforward. Once you have formed categories and subsequently re-categorized the material again and again, you could judge one piece of information against another in the same category to assess its reliability and usefulness to your research.

Preparing secondary data for analysis

Your dissertation will definitely need to address your research questions or objectives. It is likely that some or all of them may be met or answered, at least in part, by the analysis of your secondary data. It is essential, therefore, that you are able to categorize your secondary information by the research objective it is helping you to meet, or the research question it is helping to answer. This categorization should precede any attempt at analysis. It may be that you will simply sort your notes, photocopies of bits of articles, newspaper cuttings, company reports, and so on, into loose piles. For example pile (a) will help me answer my first research objective, piles (c), (d) and (e), when combined, will help me answer my second objective, and so on. Taking this approach may help you to see what else needs to be added in terms of further information, because if you have very little in one pile, it is likely to indicate that more material is needed. However do not confuse quantity with quality of information. (See Chapter 2, page 23, for some further suggestions on how to organize and to take notes from your reading.)

One problem that many business researchers have when they are beginning to analyse data is that it comes in a variety of formats. You may be faced with a pile of data relating to one broad category that originates from several academic journal articles, some foreign and domestic newspapers, a range of company reports, figures from government statistical offices and parts of documents from a variety of websites, UN bodies, and so forth. Before you can begin to analyse it, you need to reduce it to a coherent summary. Converting text and lists of words into diagrams can be a really useful way of creating summaries of data that has arrived in very different formats prior to analysis. Again, drawing diagrams such as learning maps can be excellent for linking categories of data and can be used to great effect in your dissertation. A picture really does tell a thousand words and can help to explain complex linkages in a clearer, simpler form than pages of text.

As you start to analyse your data using the categories of data you have created, you may begin to use informal methods (Collis and Hussey, 2003) to quantify your data. You need to be conscious that this is what you are doing, because it introduces judgements about the value or significance of certain bits of data. For example, if several sources have mentioned something, it may well give it greater significance in your mind than something else that has only been mentioned once. Alternatively, you may attach much greater credence to some sources than to others. As you begin to prepare your secondary data for analysis, you need to think how you could deal with this in a systematic fashion. For example, can you attach some sort of score to your various sources, according to the amount of weight you are prepared to give them? This will all form part of your evaluative judgement about the secondary data you are reading and collecting. At this stage, you just need to be very careful that the way you organize your data does not make judgements about its significance that you cannot later unravel, for example, when you have combined it with findings from your primary data collection.

Eventually, when you write your dissertation, you will want to discuss the themes you have traced in the academic literature in your literature review chapter or chapters. At this stage, you need to group your notes from your reading of the literature into these themes. These themes could be major areas such as brand extensions, family buying behaviour or employee motivation, for example, or be much more narrowly focused – it all depends on what you are trying to achieve. You need to be able to justify your choice of themes, probably by showing how significant they are in the existing academic literature.

It has been commented that Masters' students frequently expect their examiners to fill in the missing links between the data collected and the interpretation of that data. This is because many students do not make explicit their process of research and analysis. Rather than jump from coding to analysis to interpretation, you should try to create a smooth transition that demonstrates transparency in how you reached your findings. No doubt this is all clear in your head and in the conversations you may have had with your supervisor, but it may not be clear to the reader, so make sure you write it up.

Keeping Records

In order to optimize your time for analysis, you need to develop a system for recording the bibliographic information of your secondary data. Keeping accurate records of what has been read is vital, as it enables you to demonstrate how much you know about a subject and allows you to find the data again, if necessary. One important reason for having a systematic process for recording this information is that you will be able to avoid accusations of plagiarism and show that you have actually done all that reading. You may well be asked at a viva or by your examining institution to prove where your sources of information came from and you should be able to produce them. The most important issue in the early stages of data collection is to decide how you are going to record and catalogue your data. You need to keep precise and detailed bibliographic records of every document you collect or use. This is particularly important for documents found on the Internet, where you should print pages and keep as full a record as you can of the full web address of each and every document you read, and the date and the time that you read them. Some universities and colleges insist that you keep printed copies of everything that you source from the Internet and may require you to present them in a folder with your finished dissertation. It does not matter exactly how you record your bibliographic information, but it is worth thinking early on about the most efficient way that works for you. You must be disciplined about this – it will save you a massive amount of time later on. You will not want to spend too much time typing and retyping lists of references. Well-established low-tech systems include index cards, colour-coded for category, kept together in a box or a roller deck filing system. Some researchers use a Microsoft® Access® database or master lists created as Microsoft Word® documents and kept separately from the main body of work for safety.

Many people use old-fashioned card index systems, because they are flexible and easy to use. You can buy index cards in a variety of colours and a box in which to store them in most stationery shops. You can carry the cards around with you, taking them to the library and back, shuffle them about easily and sort them into temporary categories, or keep them in alphabetical order by author. You can also subdivide them into new categories that are helpful to you as you go along, invent colour codes by using different colour cards for different themes, topics or types of source, and add comments on the back of the cards to help you when you are writing about your sources of information later on. The main drawback, of course, is that at some stage you will need to transfer all this information into a word-processed format.

Electronic referencing systems are relatively easy to use but tie you into using a keyboard. EndNote® or Reference Manager® from Thomson Researchsoft for Windows® are the best known. They are expensive to buy and install yourself, but your university or college may have a software licence that enables you to use one of them on the university system. Their great advantage is that they will format a reference list for you using the data you have entered as you go along. EndNote can be used to create databases for managing references and to download references from other databases, such as Zetoc (see Chapter 5) as well as to format the reference list in your dissertation. The software will keep a list of authors, keywords and journal entries that you have previously added. Some university libraries helpfully provide lists of journals in particular subject areas in EndNote, so that you do not even need to type in the journal name when you use it.

Other students manage their bibliographic records by maintaining a master file in a separate Microsoft Word document. You can add references simply by copying and pasting all the bibliographic information from documents you are reading on the Internet into a Word file while you are searching for and downloading information. You can then transfer this to the master reference file at the end of each day. You can later edit the master reference file to form the reference list in your final dissertation. It is very important that you do edit your master list and do not simply import it into your dissertation. One of your examiners may well go through every citation you have made in the text and check that the full reference appears in the list of references. You should check very carefully that everything that you cite in the text appears in your reference list and that everything that is in your reference list is cited in the text, as it quickly becomes obvious when the two do not match up. A big disparity between the number of citations and your reference list may be taken as evidence that you have not read all the works you have cited yourself and perhaps result in the examiners accusing you of plagiarism.

Storing material

You also need to consider how you will physically store your secondary data. The paperless office has yet to become a reality – and so has the paperless researcher. You need to think about how and where you can store all your material. Student rooms are often very small and living with piles of paper on the floor can quickly become intolerable. Many researchers favour large box files, with a different one used for each main theme. Their main advantage is that they can hold lots of pieces of paper of different size. They can also be carried around on their own, though you would not want to carry more than two or three at a time. However, ten or 15 box files of paper may take up too much space in your room and the boxes themselves can be quite expensive – although they can be relabelled and used again and again.

You could invest in a filing system and file your papers alphabetically by theme or author. Cheap filing cabinets are often available from shops selling second-hand office supplies and businesses that are closing down. Plastic storage boxes, available from hardware stores, will store hanging files and are easier to move around and much lighter than filing cabinets. Your next problem is to devise a sensible filing system. Filing by author is not terribly practical when it comes to writing your literature review, as it is normally written up by theme rather than author by author. If you were researching the evolution and development of a management perspective or business area over a time period, you could file your data in date order. Otherwise, you need to establish categories and to stick to them – it is all too easy to lose documents in filing systems. Large documents, for example original newspapers, can cause problems for storage; you may need to fold or crease them to fit, roll them up or shrink them as a photocopy, while still maintaining their legibility. There will be several key journal articles or chapters of certain key text books that you will refer to over and over again and if you are moving your research from library to home and back again, it may be worth making two photocopies of these, so that you always have one to hand and also as a back-up in case of accidental damage or loss. In addition, it is easier to carry a photocopy of a chapter than a whole textbook.

Electronic storage may be particularly useful for storing numerical data that you have collected. Be careful that you enter the data consistently, as it is very easy to transpose figures and to lose sight of rows and columns when adding data (secondary or primary) to a spreadsheet. Different styles of tables from previously published research may be easier to read and compare once you have stored them in a single format. Once you have entered them into your own system, for example a Microsoft Excel® spreadsheet or SPSS® (from SPSS Inc.) software, the data will be simpler to manipulate for your own research purposes. We have found that if you are collecting a large quantity of data from an online questionnaire, you can organize the raw results to be electronically converted from the numerical replies into coded data and hold it on the Internet in a Yahoo® (or similar) email account. Later it can be electronically converted into a spreadsheet until you wish to perform your analysis. Your institution's computer services department should be able to advise you on this.

Every year we have numerous instances of students losing data through no fault of their own by fire, theft or computer crash. Flats get burgled and laptops with the only copy of the precious data on them are stolen, hard disks fail, floppy disks get corrupted, property is destroyed in fires or floods, data, entire dissertations even, go missing in the post. Always, always keep separate copies of your work, particularly if you are storing it electronically. Try and get into the habit of not only saving your work regularly while you are working but also backing it up onto a separate, removable storage disk. These now come in many forms. Floppy disks may be all that you need, but if you have a reasonable amount of graphics and tables in your files it might be better to store some on a CD. Modern computers will allow you to save large quantities of data to removable data sticks that you simply plug in to your USB port. It is now cheaper to buy one of these rather than several floppy disks. They are a useful means of transferring data from one computer to another. Most universities or colleges will have secure data storage areas that are available to students. You should back up your data file to these regularly. If a company sends you important data, make sure you have a back-up photocopy, as the organization is not likely to give you a second copy in the event of its loss or destruction.

Primary Data

Organizing your primary data into a coherent system can seem a daunting prospect, but if you are to make sense of the raw material it needs to be done. As with your secondary data, it is vital that you are very careful about keeping good records of your data collection. Audio and video tapes of interviews must be dated, numbered and labelled with the location and the people interviewed and the key topic. You must carefully record on the transcripts of interviews and focus groups and your field notes all the relevant information about the date, time, people involved and so forth. If you used any shorthand or initials, you should include a key to abbreviations, as it is amazing how difficult it can be to decipher your meaning at a later date. It is good practice to try and make notes after every interview or observation of not only who was involved, but also the possible implications for your research and any thoughts that you may have had. Some experienced researchers write a brief summary sheet that they attach to the front of each piece of primary data that records these initial impressions and some basic data about who was involved. These summaries are sometimes written on a coloured piece of paper. They can be quickly found, detached and stored together and used to form the basis of the introduction to the findings section in your dissertation.

Transcribing interviews or observation notes is a very time-consuming business and one rule of thumb is that you should estimate 6 hours of transcribing for every 1 hour of talking. The advantage of doing your own transcribing is that it allows you, the researcher, to become familiar with the raw data and prevents some errors. For example, a focus group organized by one of the authors discussed wine preferences. A secretary transcribed it as discussing 'yoghurt' rather than 'Rioja'. It is now possible to buy voice recognition software and some researchers find the reading aloud of the raw primary data into a computer helpful in familiarizing themselves with it. However, if time is pressing and financial resources allow it, transcription services through good secretarial staff are usually available in most towns, normally priced per hour or per tape.

Coding your Raw Data

Coding your data enables you to create connections between the pieces of data. While you are coding the data you can begin to conceptualize it into categories of broader meaning. By deconstructing the raw material, looking at it in detail and then re-assembling or reconstructing it into something new, it is possible to reach a deeper level of understanding about the data.

The same principles apply to coding both quantitative data and qualitative data. If you wish to analyse a closed question (a question phrased in such a way that options for answers are already given on the questionnaire), every answer option will be given a unique code, usually in the research design stage. For example, a question that asks 'rank in order of importance the factors that prevent you doing your job to the best of your ability' might give a list with all those factors. Exactly the same principle will apply to an open question, except that you have to allocate the codes subsequently, and before you can analyse the responses. For example, a question that asks 'please identify and then rank the factors that prevent you from doing your job to the best of your ability' might elicit a wide range of responses. They could be anything from 'my desk chair gives me back ache' to 'my manager does not disseminate important information'. In this case, you cannot code all the possible responses before the data is collected, as you do not know how many different responses there will be. Each time a different response is given, you must assign it a new code, while the same response will share the same code.

There are several software packages, for example NVivo™ (from ASR, the successor to NUD*IST) that will help to sort and code qualitative data for you, although some academics are sceptical about the value of this technology. The criticism levelled at these qualitative packages is that the coding mechanism cannot possibly be aware of what you are looking for and thus a 'machine'-driven coding device could have serious implications for your analysis. It has been argued that using this type of coding of qualitative data produces a 'style' of coding that is derived from grounded theory (Coffey et al., 1996), which may not have been your choice of analytical tool. However, proponents of this new technology claim it makes the process of coding easier and faster. In addition, it provides a transparent coding process and therefore offers a more explicit coding approach than was sometimes the case in past qualitative research (Bryman and Bell, 2003). If you have a small data set, which may be the case if your qualitative study is a small part of what is a mainly quantitative approach, then the use of CAQDAS (computer-aided qualitative data analysis software) such as NVivo might not be warranted. Although the successive variants of NVivo have become much more user friendly, it might not be worth learning the mechanics of such a coding system, nor will it necessarily give you any advantage over manual coding. As the coding of qualitative data is less standardized than the coding of quantitative data, you need to give a detailed discussion in your methodology about how you approached this aspect.

If pursuing qualitative research, you should aim to code your raw data as soon as possible after it has been collected. You may find that your first attempt is not as helpful as you thought it would be. Do not despair; you may recode your data several times before you see meaningful information and linkages. Coding reduces the quantity of raw data and is part of analysis but is not, in itself, analysis. When coding, you need to be consistent and it is generally more effective if you can sit down in peace and quiet and code bundles of raw data, as the process becomes easier with repetition. You need to keep a record of how you code any qualitative data and whether, during this process, you amalgamate responses that overlap or have overwhelming similarities (known as polythetic cases). As long as the processes you use are made explicit and documented, with some supporting references if at all possible, your examiners should be satisfied with your coding integrity.

There are issues surrounding coding of data. These include coding errors made in both quantitative-based and qualitative-based research, where the wrong code is assigned to a piece of data. Even a one-off error of this sort could have implications for your analysis, so checking your coding is strongly recommended. Another important issue is that by coding data you are fragmenting it and the context in which something was said or done may be lost as you break up larger pieces of raw information into tiny singular pieces. The context may be of vital importance in your research and this should not be overlooked.

Unit of analysis

Once you have successfully organized and sorted your primary and secondary data into manageable chunks of useful and relevant data, you need to consider how to analyse this valuable collection. Research methodology texts often fail to mention 'units of analysis', but it is necessary to think about this term. What does this mean in relation to your dissertation? Some authors consider the unit of analysis to be 'the thing about which data is collected' (De Vaus, 2001: 18), which might include people or organizations. However, we feel that a unit of analysis is the way that you choose to analyse your data.

You may have decided to use a particular model or framework from an academic journal article or text against which to evaluate your data, in which case the elements of that model will be the units of analysis. For example, a model on new market entry may contain elements such as product fit and so you would use 'product fit' as one heading for your analysis. Perhaps you have chosen Porter's value chain and therefore the activities within the value chain, for example 'operations', 'service', 'technology development', would become your headings for discussion.

Alternatively, you may take the main themes you found in your critical literature review as your 'units' or headings for analysis and discussion. For example, you may be trying to identify the factors of trust for online purchasing and your academic literature search may have highlighted issues such as shopping situation, previous product knowledge or personality type as key, often repeated themes. Therefore you should use those themes as your basis for analysis.

A third option for your 'units of analysis' is to analyse and discuss your data under the research questions or hypotheses that you set out in your introduction. This may help the clarity of the discussion, but in some cases it can lead to a rather narrow, boxed-in discussion where linkages and threads of discussion of the wider topic are lost.

It is also possible, although less common, to use main themes that come out of your primary data collection as your 'units of analysis'. If, for example, when interviewing employees within different organizations, interviewees keep mentioning the topics of 'emotional labour' or 'feeling pressured to perform actions that go beyond my job description' (which could be coded as 'implied pressure'), then these could be used as two headings for your analysis.

Practical Worked Example

Organizing Data

Working title: Competitive strategy in a declining market: How can a fast food retailer increase their market share of the under 6-year-old children's market in the UK?

The secondary data was collected and categorized under these headings: company information internal and external; sector information; external influencing information (for example coverage of food scares in the quality press and Department of Health information); academic literature focusing on competitive strategy and promotions aimed at children; research methods' information, including material on how to conduct primary research with very young children, and the problems associated with getting responses.

The primary research material was collected and categorized under the following headings: focus group transcripts of spoken responses; video footage of interactions of games played and role playing; pictorial data of the children's favourite foods. Additional primary data was collected through interviews with marketing managers, and advertising agency account managers for the fast food retailer. This was transcribed from Dictaphone tapes.

The student's raw qualitative data was coded manually across the data collection tools used in order to ease the process of analysis. Thus, the pictures drawn of specific favourite foods and brands were given codes and when the responses from the focus group transcripts also mentioned the same favourite food and brand, this was also given the same code as the pictures. When marketing managers mentioned the same foods and brands, the same code was used again. In this way large undigestible chunks of data begin to be broken down into smaller, more manageable pieces. The units of analysis used in this case were the themes the researcher had identified in her literature review. These themes were brand recognition, food preferences, colour, toys given away, age at which the child responded to promotions, activities, occasions. The analysis and subsequent discussion was then related back to the specific objectives of the study.

Summary

This chapter has outlined the reasons for organizing and sorting collections of data. Suggestions have been made for ways of achieving a structured system of both secondary and primary material in order to maximize the effectiveness of your subsequent analysis.

Suggested Activity

There are many different ways to break up groups of anything. Open up your wardrobe or cupboard at home and look at all your clothes: how many different ways can you categorize your clothes? Can you do it by colour, type, material, season? Note down all your different categories. From this list of categories can you identify any overlapping groups that could be put together? Can you distil your categories any further? You should now have a smaller list than you started with. Could you then justify to one of your friends why each category of the remaining list should be left in?

This activity should help you by practising how to break up data into smaller groups and think about different ways of categorizing data for clarity. There are various ways of doing this, so try several before deciding on a way that suits you and your research project.

Discussion Questions

1   What are the benefits of structuring your collected data before the analysis stage?

2   Discuss the different ways of breaking your data into units of analysis.

Further Reading

Bryman, A. and Bell, E. (2003) *Business Research Methods.* **Oxford: OUP.** See Chapter 19. This is one of the few textbooks that discusses categorizing information in a readable way.

Reflection – How to Learn to Be a Better Researcher and Business Manager from Doing Research

How Do I Show My Development as a Researcher and as an Independent Thinker?

The aim of this chapter is to show you that research is both an iterative process – it does not proceed in a straight line – and a learning process – the more you do, the better at it you will get. Many, if not most, Masters' courses require you to be 'reflective' in your written work. Increasingly, they are going further than that and asking you to produce personal development journals and pieces of reflective writing that are incorporated in your dissertation or assessed alongside it. These should document your learning experience and demonstrate your learning from it. You should in any case be able to reflect on the process of researching and writing your dissertation and be able to draw conclusions about your approach to the task and what you learned from doing it. Acquiring and developing the habit of reflection will also be very helpful in your future career. This chapter will explain how to get started as a reflective learner, how to develop your reflective skills both as a researcher and also in the workplace, and how to apply these skills to your personal development plan.

What Does it Mean to be 'Reflective'?

The ability to make reflective judgements is suggested by some authors (see Moon, 1999: Chapter 1) as the highest stage of intellectual development you can reach. Even Socrates is reported to have said, 'the unexamined life is not worth living' (Plato, *Apology*, line 38a). The basic idea of reflection is to hold up a mirror to something you have done, to analyse the process and to think about what you learned from it. There is a lot of academic writing about reflection (see the Further Reading at the end of this chapter for some suggestions about what to look at) and it can be made to sound extremely complex. There is considerable debate even about how to define reflection. The main point about it, though, is that it is a mental process directed to a specific purpose or an outcome that enables you to learn from experience. So it needs to be both structured in some way and to be recorded.

Why is it Important to Learn How to Reflect?

Acquiring the ability to reflect is important because it shows that you can learn from experience, deal with uncertainty, and think about your own role in the construction of knowledge. In your working life you will be constantly faced with having to make decisions about things, frequently rather unexpectedly and on the basis of partial or incomplete knowledge of the issues. You will be asked to use your own critical judgement in order to make these decisions. It is a very good idea to start developing this ability while you are studying. Because skills in self-management are essential both in your studies and in later life, gaining an insight into how you learn and how to improve your performance will give you greater independence and confidence in your judgements. You also need to have a good understanding of yourself in order to work effectively with other people, and it is useful if you have been forced to think and develop strategies for doing this while you are still studying. That is one reason why the Dearing (1997) report into the future of higher education in the UK recommended that universities enable students to monitor, build and reflect on their personal development, and why this is now a requirement on all undergraduate courses.

Getting Started

Reflection in the workplace

If you are studying for an MBA or DMS, or if you are on a placement as part of your course, you will undoubtedly be required to reflect on your experience in the workplace. Two types of reflection are sometimes distinguished, though in reality the boundaries between them can be a bit fuzzy. The first is reflection while you are taking part in decisions (sometimes called reflection-in-action) (Schön, 1983; Moon, 1999). The second type of reflection is reflection in hindsight, and is sometimes termed reflection-on-action. In practice, reflection-in-action is very hard to describe and to capture and record in a meaningful way, as much of it consists of the application of tacit knowledge that is never openly acknowledged or formalized. You are much more likely to be asked to reflect with a degree of hindsight.

Getting into the habit of reflection-on-action while you are a student of business and management is a way of developing your skills as a reflective practitioner, which is a core management skill, but one that is difficult to teach and very hard to learn in a classroom and divorced from practice. Many of the more vocational courses taken on a part-time basis by students in full-time employment, such as the postgraduate diplomas in management or human resource development, already include a requirement to keep a learning log (Barclay, 1996). Reflective practice involves reflecting on your own practice in the workplace, and on the context or setting in which it occurs. It may be about your continuing role or about a specific event or unexpected issue. The main characteristics of reflective practice in the workplace include the following:

- **The reflection should be about something that is uncertain and has no immediate solution.**

- **It should have a strong critical element.**

- **The result is as likely to be a better understanding as much as a resolution of a problem.**

- **The general aim should be to improve practice in future.**

- **The immediate aim may be self-development or empowerment.**

- **There can be an emotional dimension to reflection and you may need to acknowledge this.**

- **Sharing your reflection with others may enhance the learning that you get from it.**

(Adapted from Moon, 1999)

Recording your reflections

Once you have reached a working definition of reflection, and appreciated the need to do it, the next point to consider is how to record it. Your mental processes are private, but for the purposes of demonstrating that you have engaged in reflection, you need to record them in written form eventually. Keeping an audio diary might be a good way of capturing passing thoughts and impressions and it is possible to keep a video diary as well, but at some stage you will still need to transcribe them.

It is perhaps not surprising that the best way to capture and present reflection is another area for debate, but universities and colleges usually ask for one of the following:

- **learning logs;**

- **personal development plans;**

- **reflective diaries;**

- **progress files;**

- **learning or reflective journals;**

- **researcher's journals.**

In addition, or sometimes as an alternative, you may just be asked to include some reflection on the learning process, or some reflective writing in your project or dissertation. Evidence of reflection may be one of the criteria on which your work will be assessed. It is up to you and your teachers to make sure that you understand exactly what the particular requirements of your course are and that you have met them.

Unless your course regulations insist that you do something different, one of the best ways of recording your process of reflecting on your professional practice is to keep a reflective journal or diary. The journal is not a portfolio of professional achievements or 'problems that I have overcome' but is an ongoing management development document. You can also use a reflective journal to document your development as a researcher.

You will probably have been asked to fill in a skills profile as part of your course or placement. Writing a reflective journal may enable you to identify learning as it takes place. You can then use it to update your skills matrix or profile towards the end of your course. You can also use reflective journals to record an experience, which may in itself be useful to log, for example, how you went about conducting an interview. However, merely logging the experience can limit the usefulness of the journal. Just recording what you did in the course of a day's work or a day's research is not enough. You need to reflect on what was happening and to identify the learning that has taken place. From that process, you can then further reflect on your personal skills and how they are developing and if necessary start to identify areas that need further work.

Writing a reflective journal or diary can be viewed as a tool for teaching yourself, which, with practice, can become embedded into your own personal cycle of learning. The journal can develop into an important learning tool during the process of becoming a competent researcher. The process of reflecting on what happened should enable you to learn from the consequences and then to move forward with an action plan to help you. Using reflection in this way makes you become your own agony aunt and if you apply it to your own research, thoughts and activities it will help your development as a researcher. Being able to apply your reflection to management activities that you might then alter if you were faced with a similar situation again takes reflective journals from being an internal self-diagnostic tool to an external management tool.

How Do I Go About Writing a Reflective Journal?

It is sometimes helpful to ask yourself questions when you start the process of reflection. For example, you could ask yourself 'what was my best achievement this week (or today) as a researcher or postgraduate student?' Once you have identified an achievement, the next stage is to think how you could improve upon that. Another way is to think about an issue that you felt you did not handle particularly well in your studies. If your work or research has involved interactions with others, perhaps you should consider if there were aspects of these interactions that you were not happy with, and how you could have handled them differently.

The process of reflection needs to be broken up into discrete tasks in order for you to think about your activities in a systematic and helpful way. One framework that we have found useful is to work through the following headings, which we have adapted from a book by Gibbs:

- **Description: what actually happened?**

- **Feelings: what I felt about what happened**

- **Evaluation: was it a positive or negative experience?**

- **Analysis: what sense can I make of the experience, where does it fit within my personal development?**

- **Conclusion: what else could I have done?**

- **Action plan: in a similar situation what would I do now?**

(Developed from Gibbs, 1988)

It can be helpful to practice this technique on something that is not related to your research or your work in order to understand the process better. Here is an example of breaking down the components of an activity, using the headings, and reflecting upon it so as to develop an action plan that might enable you to benefit from the experience.

Practical Worked Example

Reflective Journal

- **Description** – I got up, ate three bowls of cereal because I was hungry, and then, owing to my longer than usual breakfast, missed the bus to get me to my lecture on time. Fortunately a friend with a car saw me waiting at the bus stop and offered me a lift!
- **Feelings** – I was full from breakfast, frustrated that I had missed the bus and relieved and grateful that my friend offered me a lift.
- **Evaluation** – The early morning journey started off as a negative experience but luckily ended as a positive one, and I am fortunate to have a helpful friend.
- **Analysis** – This experience indicates that I should eat more sensibly, plan my time better and make sure that I appreciate my friends.
- **Conclusion** – I could have eaten more dinner the night before, I could have got up earlier if I was going to have a longer breakfast, I could have left my house in time to catch the bus, I could have looked at the bus timetable, I could have organized a lift to university the day before, etc.
- **Action plan** – Having had the experience, I will organize my time better by planning what I have to do and when I have to be somewhere and writing this up on a timetable. I will also buy an alarm clock to help me get up in the mornings on time and I will buy a bicycle so that I can cycle to university. I will also cook my friend a meal to say thank you. In the longer term I will try to get a job over the next vacation so that I will finally have enough money in 6 months to buy my own car and then not have to rely on other people for transport.

What format should a journal be in?

Reflective journals can take several forms and there is no one method of writing them. It is important that you devise something that works for you and is as easy as possible for you to record; otherwise you are not likely to continue with it. One method that we have found that can work quite well is to combine a log of events on one side of the page with your reflections about that event on the other side of the page. A further column could also be added, perhaps at a later date, that incorporates your reflection on your initial reflection and what you might do about it. This should capture the learning from the process and possibly some action points for you to think about or put into effect now or at a later, specified date.

Another approach is to use different colours for different aspects of your work or different roles. You may have different sections of a diary for different elements of your life. Some researchers keep a small notebook, while others create a Microsoft Word document or even a Microsoft Excel spreadsheet to use as a framework. You may keep an electronic diary on a shared drive if you are researching as part of a group, as ideas and thoughts and reflections can be quickly and easily shared via email. Any system that works for you is appropriate, as these journals are individual, but you should try to stick with one method that you can feel happy with.

How often should I write in it?

In order to capture your ideas and feelings, reflective journals should be written up as close to the event as possible, together with your thoughts about that event. You can then return to your writing at a later stage and add in further reflection when it comes to you. In science subjects, researchers often note down reflections after every set of experiments. As a business and management researcher, you should consider writing a daily reflective journal. Committing the initial reactions to paper is as important as writing a more considered review later on, as you need a starting point.

Who else should see it?

These journals can be kept as entirely private documents for your eyes only, in which case they are closer to being confessional diaries. You may choose to share some of the content with other researchers, or with your supervisor as a basis for a focused discussion on one particular aspect of your dissertation or project. If you are using your reflective journal as a management development tool, you may wish to show your diary to your line manager to make a point or to initiate a conversation. Extracts from your reflective journal may be useful in your dissertation, as part of assessed course work, as part of a personal development plan (see later in this chapter) or to fulfil a requirement of your assessed work. Keeping up your journal requires considerable self-discipline, so it is really up to you to use the resource as effectively as you can.

Using a Reflective Journal when Doing Research

Reinterpreting ideas and concepts and linking theory to practice are essential components of good research and a reflective journal is an ideal mechanism for capturing the process of reflection that leads you to draw conclusions of this type. There are a number of other tangible, positive benefits of keeping a reflective journal or researcher's diary when you are carrying out your research. These range from providing documentary evidence for your supervisor that you have actually carried out the research, to providing part of a record of the data you collected during the research. When carrying out participant observation, for example, you must try to write up a reflection on what went on during your participant observation later on, so a contemporary, or near contemporary, record that you can draw on is invaluable.

One of the most interesting things you can do when you start your dissertation is to write down, in note form, what you expect the outcomes to be. You can then put that piece of paper away until after the work has been completed, possibly until after the dissertation has been bound and submitted. As an experienced researcher, you will then be able to look back over your work and see whether the outcome came anywhere near the original notes on the piece of paper. The similarities, or indeed contrasts, are likely to give you insight into your own preconceptions about research and may even be amusing. This piece of paper may even be of help earlier. It might be worth getting it out when you have got to the stage in your dissertation when you are reflecting on the research process, as it can enable you to give an honest assessment of what you have learned during the process and what you might do differently now you have gained that self-knowledge.

You can facilitate your own learning from the experience of working on an assignment or writing a dissertation by adding notes in your journal or diary that reflect on the experience you are going through as a researcher. Areas worth exploring in a reflective journal include what you actually feel like when you are doing your research and why that might be. For example, you might record how you felt before and during a research interview you were carrying out with a participant. Were you anxious to start with and, if so, why was that? Might it have been because you had not done enough preparation, or were you nervous about meeting someone with an important management role in an organization? You could add what you might do to change the interview experience for the next time you conducted one. By writing down what happened, what you felt at the time, and what you might do differently next time, a valuable slowing down process takes place, which helps you, the researcher, to have a more thorough understanding of the elements of what occurred. These are both internal (within you) and external (the event itself) (Christensen, 1981). Using reflective journals when you are involved in group research is also likely to enhance the outcome, as long as the whole group participates in keeping a diary or journal (Walker, 1985).

By keeping a reflective journal while you are doing your research, you may find yourself able to solve problems relating to your research. For example, you may be undertaking an inductive piece of research, but your underlying belief is that deductive, hypothesis testing and theory proving is 'better'. A diary may illustrate this dichotomy for you and enable you to resolve the contradiction. Keeping a journal may even enhance your creativity.

If you have notes on what you did previously and your reflections about that experience, you might come up with an innovative idea, as associations and linkages may emerge from the written page. By practising reflection on your activities in the form of a journal, you are also likely to improve your critical thinking and reading abilities (see Chapter 6). If you question what you read and the information bombarding your senses, you may find that you develop a deeper understanding of all your material.

Some students find that keeping a reflective diary helps them to build confidence in their abilities as a researcher. Reflective writing helps you to find out how you yourself go about learning and this enhances independence of thought and action. Both personal development journals and reflective journals are also useful in helping the process and flow of writing. Writing can help to clarify your thoughts and you get better at writing through constant practice (see Chapter 10). These records can act as a private or public voice of your thoughts, problems, ideas and developing abilities as a researcher. Don't worry if writing about your feelings about the stages you are going through in your learning does not come easily to you at first. The more often you jot things down, the easier it is to chart your development as a competent researcher.

Incorporating Reflection in your Dissertation

Within the dissertation, there are numerous ways to demonstrate your development as a competent, reflective researcher. In your methodology chapter, for example, you can demonstrate how you came to choose the research method(s) you eventually selected, why you rejected possible alternative approaches and why with hindsight this was justified. How rigorously you applied your chosen methods will also give the marker many clues as to how considered your research process was. In your discussion of the range of data sources that you used and in the justification that you write for what you included or excluded, you will again be able to show your considered reflective approach to data collection and evaluation.

Any anomalies in your results or initial attempts at analysis that were not satisfactory should be reported honestly in your dissertation (see Chapter 10). They will help to illustrate your ability to face problems and to solve them creatively. A discussion in your dissertation of how you would approach the same project if doing it again, perhaps with more resources, and what you would do differently if you had this opportunity, will clearly indicate how deeply you have thought about these issues, and you are likely to be given credit for this.

Outside the boundaries of the finished dissertation, many researchers use personal development journals or reflective journals for reflective development (see section on reflection in the workplace earlier in this chapter). These tools are seen as aids to management development, as the ability to reflect and learn from decision-making and its consequences can assist in a manager's performance.

Reflective Journals as an Aid to Professional Practice

One of the problems with being a manager is that there is a tendency to get immersed in day-to-day issues. You might deal with them on an ad-hoc basis, and you may never get around, or have the time, to think about whether there are any underlying patterns or problems that require a change in your professional practice. For example, if you are a sales manager, you might spend a lot of your time dealing with sales targets, regional sales patterns and monitoring sales force performance. You might never get round to thinking about why one member of your team outperforms the others or why you don't get the support from the service department that you feel is needed, or what the longer-term consequences are of a set of decisions you made.

If you could keep a reflective journal, either by recording your thoughts on a casette tape, or by setting 10 minutes aside and jotting some down, using the headings given earlier in this chapter (Feelings, Evaluation, Analysis, Conclusion, Action plan), you could readily identify a number of key issues where there is no immediate solution. You then need to decide which are the most important to deal with in the longer term. You could use the questions below to prompt your own reflection on your professional practice, with the aim of developing the learning to enable you to begin to suggest possible solutions.

- **What was I trying to achieve?**

- **Why did I do what I did?**

- **What were the consequences of my action?**

- **How did I feel about it?**

- **How did those around me feel about it?**

- **How do I know that?**

- **What internal factors influenced my decision?**

- **What external factors influenced my decision?**

- **What other information should I have had to make a decision?**

- **Could I have done it better?**

- **What other choices did I have?**

- **How do I feel about it now?**

(Adapted from Moon, 1999)

Many areas of work require people to be what are sometimes described as 'reflective practitioners' (Cottrell, 2003) and this is good management practice whether or not it is an explicit requirement of your course. Broadly, it means that you have to take personal responsibility for your own professional development, which means that you need to identify ways of using your own strengths in the work that you do, and also to identify areas that you should improve by undertaking training and study. You also need to recognize and take responsibility for the effects of your own behaviour at work and to work out how you can make a useful contribution to team efforts. Reflection is a key tool to enable you to do this.

Personal Development Plans

A personal development plan (PDP) is a set of records that you make and maintain. They should include what you have learned as you have progressed through your education at university and a record of your marks. They are much more than just grade cards, however; their purpose is to enable you to reflect on what you have learned and to plan your future learning. They tend to focus on how you have developed skills that are essential to your future life such as teamwork, problem-solving and self-management, as well as on academic achievement. A PDP can be written in any style you feel comfortable with, but your university may have a preferred format. A PDP may focus on listing specific skills or techniques that you have learned that help you with your research or that will be useful in future or current work. For example, you may discuss how you learned a specific statistical analysis software tool or how to moderate a focus group. It may also contain notes to yourself about problematic research questions and breakthroughs you reached with them.

PDPs are often based on an evaluation of your own strengths and weaknesses. One way to start is to perform a SWOT (strengths, weaknesses, opportunities and threats) analysis on yourself (Cottrell, 2003). You could do this at the beginning, during and at the end of your course. You can also do this before, during and after your Masters' dissertation, to see how you have developed as a researcher. A SWOT analysis on yourself is done in the same way as a SWOT analysis of a business organization. In just the same way, it asks you to identify your own strengths and weaknesses as a Masters' student, and then to analyse external opportunities and threats. You can ask yourself questions such as 'am I organized?' Or 'what is my time management like?' Once you have conducted a SWOT analysis for your PDP that lists your strengths, weaknesses, opportunities and threats, you can begin to identify gaps that could be filled in terms of skills or knowledge. Your focus here should be on how your SWOT relates to your ability as a researcher.

During your time at university, you will receive regular feedback from experts in a way that you will rarely experience again (Cottrell, 2003). This comes in the form of comments on your submitted work. University teachers spend hours writing feedback on student work only to see that work uncollected or the remarks ignored. Of course, not all feedback is helpful, but you should try to swallow your pride and use what you have been given as a basis for some positive reflective learning. The first and most important point is to read it and then to re-read it a few days later, when perhaps you can be more objective about the comments. Do you agree with the comments and were they the sort of comments that you had expected? If you do not agree with them, why is this? Have you had similar comments in the past and, if so, why was this? Work through the Feelings, Evaluation, Analysis, Conclusion, Action plan framework described earlier in the chapter. Record this in your PDP together with a copy of the feedback sheet or note of the feedback you were given. What actions can you take to improve your performance? Do you need to get some clarification from the person who gave the feedback? Book an appointment to go and see them. Are there books, web pages, support services or courses that you could get access to in order to address some of the issues? At the end of each semester, or term, or the beginning of the next one, when you may be feeling less tired and more optimistic, read through all the previous term's feedback and identify any common themes. Draw up an action plan to enable you to deal with them.

Practical Worked Example

A Researcher's Journal

5 June

Am anxious about trying to analyse all my raw data, am not sure where or how to start – I guess this is only because I have never done anything like this before. I am normally quite good at problem-solving, so I shall try to come up with three ideas for how to approach my data analysis and then go and discuss these with my supervisor. Last time she was very helpful and we found a way forward.

10 June

Some progress at last! Supervisor suggested some reading and further thinking, so having read several bits of books on content analysis I tried it for the first time on a few bits of my raw data. I think it might work and may partially help answer one of my research questions. It seems quite straightforward to apply.

14 June

Have run into problems with making up consistent rules for my content analysis but am writing every variation down, so at least I know what I did last time. I wonder if by using content analysis I will be able to create the categories I need?

16 June

I seem to have far too many categories. How on earth do I reduce them? What do the books say? Have been to see my supervisor and she suggested asking someone else to help me amalgamate the categories. I thought this was cheating! She said it was accepted practice in qualitative research to get people to make separate judgements and then to see the extent of their agreement. Of course, I remember I read about it in a research study … can't remember which one, at the moment. Need to look at some more methods books.

Practical Worked Example

Reflection on Feedback Using Prompt Questions

What do I feel about this feedback? Very helpful feedback. Makes clear how important it is to think about the task that has been set before I actually write the coursework paper.

What do I think about this feedback? Very useful in pointing out flaws in my work that could be eliminated in future assignments. It clearly states my strengths and my weaknesses and points me in the direction of successfully completing future work.

Based on this feedback, what actions could I take to improve my work for another assignment? Look at more journal articles – improve my search skills – course? Need to find articles that present different views in order to develop an argument, and need to identify both classical and contemporary views so I can be sure what current thinking is.

Reflection after Completing your Dissertation

Once you have finished writing and have submitted your dissertation, you will probably feel greatly relieved. You may feel that you never wish to think about your chosen subject again and would prefer to move swiftly on to the next episode in your life. However, in terms of your own personal development it is worth pausing to reflect. How did you cope with being a researcher, were there elements that made you uncomfortable? Was it difficult for you to be assertive in getting permission within an organization? Were you uneasy about interviewing strangers? Did the reliance on technology in the form of SPSS (the statistical analysis software package, see Chapter 7) take you outside your comfort zone? Was being a researcher a role that came easily to you or are you still more comfortable being an employee?

If you take the time to reflect after your research has ended as well as during the process, you may learn how you have altered from the experience. You might have learned specific new skills such as data analysis; alternatively you might have gained confidence in the value of your own opinion. It is useful to reflect on how being involved in management research might have changed you and what insight you have gained about yourself from this experience. Conducting research may have been so engrossing that you wish to do more, either singularly or as a collaborative researcher working with those publishing in your specialism. Your chosen subject area may have become so interesting to you that you wish to take your research further and register for a PhD. Before taking the next step in your career, set aside some time to consider the highs and lows of being a researcher and whether you are suited to it.

Summary

This chapter has explored the value of being able to reflect on what you have done and how that improves your effectiveness as a researcher and as an employee. Different methods of demonstrating your reflective abilities have been outlined, both within the written dissertation itself and also through the use of reflective journals and PDPs.

Suggested Activity

Think of something that happened to you this week. Ask yourself the following questions: How do I feel about this event? What do I think about this event? What can I do in the future based on my reflection on this event?

Using the headings suggested earlier in the chapter (Feelings, Evaluation, Analysis, Conclusion, Action plan), write down an event that relates to your research activities and use the headings to reflect upon the event. What have you learned from the experience itself and what have you learned from the experience of reflecting upon it?

Discussion Questions

1 How can reflection on group activities improve your interactions with others?

2 Why is it important to demonstrate reflection in your Master's dissertation?

Further Reading

Cottrell, S (2003) *Skills for Success: The Personal Development Planning Handbook.* **Basingstoke: Palgrave MacMillan.** All you need to know about how to prepare and write PDPs and the advantages of using this approach to learning.

<table>
<tr><td>

9

</td><td>

Reliability, Validity and Generalization

How Can I Tell if the Research is Any Good?

</td></tr>
</table>

Your course work and your dissertation are to some extent sales documents – you need to convince your reader or examiner of the quality of your work. This chapter helps you to make assessments about the rigour of the sources of information you have used in your literature review, the weight you can give to your secondary research, as well as the quality of your own primary research if you undertake any. In particular, we introduce you to, and then apply the concepts of, reliability, validity and the extent to which generalizations may be made. It should enable you to reach a better understanding of academic articles you may have read, as well as your own research. It is likely that you will have a whole section of a chapter or even a whole chapter devoted to a discussion of the reliability, validity and generalization of the findings of your research project.

The 'Troublesome Triplets'

Lots of students have difficulty grappling with and making sense of the rather abstract concepts of reliability, validity and generalization. As they are often put together, this has led us to call them the 'troublesome triplets' (Quinton and Smallbone, 2005), but we hope that by the time you have finished working through this chapter they will no longer be so troublesome. Students are somehow expected to know whether the research they read or carry out is rigorous and will stand up to scrutiny by other people. It is taken for granted that somewhere in your education you will have developed knowledge about how to test data for its validity, how to know the extent to which you can make generalizations from it, and how to know whether or not you can rely on it. But apart from the use of very specific statistical tests for some aspects of validity and data reliability in quantitative studies, most research methods textbooks offer very little advice on this. We hope that this chapter will help to fill the gap.

Of course, you need to unpick the triplets in a way that is appropriate to your particular project, and this chapter aims to demonstrate various techniques to help you to do this through the use of examples. Once the basic principles are understood and applied, the concepts of reliability, validity and level of generalization should no longer make you fearful.

Validity, reliability and generalization apply as much to other people's research as they do to your own. Working through Chapter 6 on critical reading will have enabled you to sharpen your critical faculties when it comes to assessing the worth of other published research, particularly academic journal articles. The suggestions in this chapter should help you to probe further into the underpinning research and to make judgements about how good you think it is.

Your decisions about your research design, and the research methods you are going to use in your research, will determine to a considerable extent which of several different approaches to validity, reliability and the extent to which research findings can be generalized to other cases or populations you will choose. Your underlying research approach or philosophy (see Chapter 1) will also affect how you view the triplets. In this chapter, we start with an introductory discussion of some of the main definitions of reliability, validity and generalization. Sections that deal with how these abstract concepts can and should be applied to both secondary and primary research follow.

Validity

Much of the past thinking about the validity of research designs in the social sciences, of which business research is one, comes from thinking about the validity of experimental research in chemistry and biology. Management research draws for its philosophical approach and research methodology from social science research, and as with the experimental tradition this has tended to be positivist and deductive in its past orientation. Four tests or types of validity are commonly used (Yin, 2003) and you may well come across these in academic writing. They are internal validity, construct validity, external validity and reliability. The guidance given to the researcher is not always very clear, as different authors split validity up in different ways. For example, Cooper and Schindler (2003), who are concerned mainly with quantitative research and statistical testing, divide internal validity into three different parts. This makes it all very confusing for researchers. The really important point about validity for your work is that you must make clear to whoever is assessing your work that the rigour of your approach and your thinking about it is transparent. So you should discuss this in your work – perhaps in your chapter or section on research methods and maybe again when you are drawing conclusions and discussing the limitations to your work.

Internal validity

The methodological roots in the experimental sciences helps to explain why a commonly given explanation of the term internal validity is whether what you actually measured was what you intended to measure, when the research was designed. An example of a student project whose research design lacked internal validity, before even starting on the data collection, was a business project whose objective was to measure the differences in brand equity between two automotive manufacturers. The initial primary research design suggested asking the general public about their car brand preferences. In this case, the proposed method would not generate the answers that would help to meet the research objective. Although the respondents may have given their preferences in terms of car brands, their responses would not have directly helped to measure differences in brand equity between the two firms. Thus this proposed project had no internal validity.

The key test of validity is therefore sometimes presented as 'was what was found a response to the questions originally asked?' Some authors describe this as being face validity (Collis and Hussey, 2003), others as internal validity, yet others as measurement validity (Saunders et al., 2003). You can see how important it is to get this right when you are doing an experiment that is designed to test or prove a hypothesis. If you are doing a quantitative study, your tests of internal validity will probably focus on causality. Your test might be how confident you are that the independent variable is at least partly responsible for the variation found in the dependent variable (Bryman and Bell, 2003). For example, you might carry out an experiment to see if moving a point of sale promotion (a gondola in a shop containing discounted products for instance) closer to the till raises or lowers sales. The change in the position of the gondola is your independent variable. You might compare the results from one till with those from another, where the gondola has not been moved, and measure the outcome by looking at the receipts on both tills both before and after the intervention. The till receipts provide the evidence you need about any impact on the level of sales, which is your dependent variable. In your research design, you would need to make allowances and, if possible, control external variables that would affect your results, such as the time of day, the day of the week, the weather and other promotions running in store. If you were happy that you had managed to do this, then you could be confident that your experiment had internal validity and that you had demonstrated the cause of any variation in till receipts. You could carry out statistical tests to help to confirm this.

Suppose, however, that the initial purpose of the research could not be answered because the data actually collected answered a rather different question. Perhaps the extent and type of customer interaction with staff was a key issue in the sales variations that you measured, and you did not realise this until later. In this case, your research would lack internal validity. Textbooks on quantitative methods, in particular, have lots to say about the many threats to internal validity. Subsequent researchers have expanded the list of threats to internal validity in experimental research originally distinguished by Campbell and Stanley in 1963 (cited in Cooper, 1998). If your research design is based around an experiment, which is quite rare in Masters' dissertations but may be more common in some areas such as hospitality and retail, and you hope to get statistical data, you will need to discuss these in more detail in you methods chapter or section.

If your approach is much more inductive (see Chapter 1), you are unlikely to be too worried about internal validity in the way it was defined above, because you will be trying to approach your research in as open a way as possible, without rigid preconceived ideas. So from your point of view, if your research data answers a question that is slightly different from how you thought it might turn out, that is no cause for alarm. Internal validity is sometimes seen as a particular strength of qualitative research in general, because you collect so much data that it must in itself be sufficient to tell you something about the subject of study.

In terms of recently published business research methods textbooks, Cooper and Schindler (2003) may be taken as exemplars of the positivist approach to business research. In Chapter 8 of their book, they discuss methods of evaluating a research tool used for 'scientific measurement' (p. 231) in terms of its internal validity, reliability and practicality. Practicality is defined as economy – which is almost always an issue for a researcher – convenience (for the respondent) and interpretability. Unfortunately, their guidance to the novice researcher on aspects of validity is not always very clear. For example, they subdivide internal validity into three aspects. The first is content validity – the test is, does the measure adopted fit the data that is to be or has been collected? This is an issue of judgement and they suggest the designer of the research and an independent panel of experts can best judge it. This is of little practical use to a Masters' student, but if you are collecting quantitative data, your supervisor or research methods teacher should be able to advise you about its likely content validity. The student project on brand equity described above never actually started because the student had feedback at an early stage that you could not measure brand equity in this way.

Cooper and Schindler (2003) also discuss what they describe as criterion-related validity – the success of the measure in predicting an outcome. For example, opinion polls may be used to predict the outcome of an election (predictive validity), or correctly to categorize something, such as who supports hunting (concurrent validity). In practice, they suggest, this may be difficult to validate, with the researcher able only to use other secondary data. If you are predicting an outcome, you can of course, wait to see if it happens, but that may not be much help to you in submitting your dissertation on time. If the secondary data is so good that you can use it to validate your primary data, it is arguable that you should not be doing the new research in the first place. Their third category of internal validity is construct validity, which is to do with the inherent validity of the theory you are testing. But they do not offer much help in how to assess it, suggesting that it is an abstract concept, which makes it harder to validate, and that the researcher needs to consider the theory and the measure together.

External validity

A second aspect of validity, external validity, is an assessment of whether the results could be applied to other contexts or situations and to what extent this may be possible. In quantitative studies, the representativeness of the sample is the key issue in generalizing to a larger population. For example, it is a fairly mind-boggling thought that a survey of the voting intentions of 2000 people can enable you to predict the outcome of an election in which 30 million will take part, but as long as the sampling has been very carefully designed and carried out, political opinion polls are now able to achieve a remarkable level of predictive accuracy. If you are generalizing from a sample to a population, there are a number of tests that you can use to try and make sure that what your sample tells you is as representative as possible of the broader population.

Although external validity was originally seen as relating to the generalizability of the research based on the rigour of the research design, subsequent studies have referred to population validity, ecological validity and added other validity parameters, such as statistical validity. The whole approach is quite problematic for anyone trying to undertake research and seeking guidance in a range of methods books. Unfortunately, different researchers use different lists of threats to validity, which they classify under different headings, and there is no established guidance as to the relative weight to be given to each of these.

Some writers do not think these criteria are ever relevant in studies that are carried out in a broadly phenomenological perspective. For example, measurement has arguably little sense in qualitative research, so it is questionable whether the issue of validity is of concern at all. The use of case studies and small samples makes it hard to generalize from qualitative research studies. Although generalizability is seldom dealt with at any length in discussions of qualitative research methods, it is important to note that some authors have actively rejected it altogether as an objective of qualitative research (Schofield, 1990).

You could approach the issue of external validity by asking how transferable the findings are to another context and whether they may even be relevant in another context. This aspect of validity is entwined with the concept of generalization and so they will be considered together after we have looked at the next of the troublesome triplets, reliability.

Reliability

Reliability is sometimes seen as an assessment of whether the same findings would be obtained if the research were repeated, or if someone else conducted it. This definition is problematic in business and management research, as any social context involving people makes replication of research very difficult (LeCompte and Goetz, 1982). In a qualitative study, such issues can be either outside the boundaries of what you need to think about when doing qualitative research or a big problem, depending on which authors you consult.

In a quantitative study, reliability is really about the consistency of your results, the robustness of the measure and whether it is free of random or unstable error. As with validity, there are statistical tests that you can carry out to assess the reliability of your findings. According to Cooper and Schindler (2003), stability, equivalence and internal consistency are key concerns. Reliability estimates, they suggest, can be of three kinds. The first is test-re-test, whereby you ask the same sample exactly the same questions again a few weeks later, looking for consistency in their responses. You can also estimate whether alternative forms of the same measure produce similar results. You can administer two different forms of your questionnaire at the same time and produce from that an estimate of how reliable or consistent your sample is in the answers they give by looking to see if you get similar results. The third test is to use what are termed split-half correlations that are measured using a statistical device called Kronbach's alpha or KR 20. This measures the degree of consistency between, say, the list of answers given by respondents in the first half of a questionnaire compared with the answers the same people gave in the second half of the same questionnaire.

The problem for you as a researcher is the emphasis in the textbooks on issues of judgement and on really rather cumbersome practices which, according to Bryman and Bell (2003), few researchers carry out in practice. Few published research reports discuss the reliability and validity of their data in the terms suggested in the methods books. When two US academics (Podsakoff and Dalton, 1987) looked at published quantitative research in the top journals in their field of organization studies, only 3 percent of the articles they reviewed provided any evidence of tests for validity. However, this is not an option you should follow in your dissertation or assignments. The examiners will be looking for evidence that you have assessed your data for, and can comment on, its validity and reliability, and the extent to which you can and do make generalizations based on what you have read and researched.

You can improve or strengthen the reliability of your research by:

- **using differing data sources;**

- **using different data collection tools;**

- **applying established theory from one area to another;**

- **collecting data at different time points;**

- **using different researchers at different points of the research.**

For example, if you used only a couple of interviews with key informants and based your analysis on those interviews, and did not provide a clear and well supported argument for how you went about your primary research and why your data sources were so limited, your work would be said to have severely limited reliability. This would cast huge doubt over your findings. On the other hand, if you were looking at, for example, crisis management and managed to achieve interviews with only two managers in different organizations who had significant personal experience in this area, you could greatly add to the reliability of your findings from the interviews. You could carry out a cross-analysis on the basis of extensive research into crisis management using secondary data and academic sources by using data from these sources both to inform your interviews and to cross-check your notes of the interviewees' answers. You could also carry out an assessment of the significance of their experience by referring to the type of industry they are in and their role within it.

You should check the description of the research method used in any academic article you read or source of secondary data. Did the author use some or any of the techniques stated above in the data collection phase of the research? Evidence of triangulation such as using several different data collection tools, for example conducting observations and a survey, or incorporating a real breadth of secondary sources will add strength to any findings. You should look for this when reading other people's work as a way of assessing the rigour of their research.

In your own research design, have you ensured that you are using more than one data collection tool in order to add credence to your findings? Using different data collection tools to answer the same research question is known as 'triangulation' and is expected in postgraduate research. By incorporating multiple research tools to answer the same research question, you are providing a stronger body of evidence for the examiner or audience of your project. Triangulation may help to reinforce your findings, as, in the example above, when both the results from the observations and the questionnaires agree with each other.

Alternatively, triangulation may throw up differences in the findings, which should then be investigated further. For example, asking people about their supermarket shopping habits may provide data that is different from what you observed in supermarkets, leading you to conclude that people say different things from how they actually behave. In this case, however, you do not really have sufficient evidence on its own to support this conclusion, and it does not help you to answer the interesting question as to why this might be so. You may have to revisit your research question, carry out further primary research using a third data collection tool, and return to the academic literature to search for clues that can help you to draw reliable conclusions (see Figure 9.1).

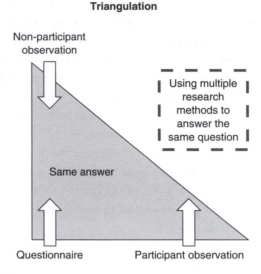

Triangulation

Figure 9.1   Triangulation

Generalization

A common problem for students at different levels is the extent to which their findings may be applied to another context. We probably all like to think that our research is going to shed new light on some difficult general research problem or can lead to a key theory being revised or over-turned. Generalization is the extent to which you can come to a conclusion about one thing, based on information about another (Vogt, 1993). For example, does your study of a single company in the fashion sector enable you to make generalizations about issues you know are common to that sector, or to a different sector, or to the clothing industry in general, to manufacturing or creative industries or to the fashion sector worldwide?

The discussion about the extent and appropriateness of generalization is an ongoing debate among academics, so you should not be worried over conflicting views that you might have read. The 'yes, generalizations can be made from a few in depth, data-rich samples' camp includes authors such as Norman (1970) and Gummeson (1991). The 'we are doubtful about the ability to generalize based on limited research' camp includes Creswell (2003) and Bryman and Bell (2003). You should aim to be open and honest about the scope, potential and limitations of your research by stating explicitly what these might be, rather than waiting for someone to find the chinks in your research armour. However, in our experience, students do appear to over generalize the results of their research and you need to try to avoid this.

As a researcher, perhaps the first question you should think about is whether you need to generalize from your own work at all? If you are undertaking exploratory research, generalization may not be part of your intended outcome. For example, you may wish to focus your research on identifying certain personality traits in cross-cultural management teams and whether these may impact on the effectiveness of the team. But your research may be limited to a literature review and an exploratory study of one such team. It is not always necessary to 'try' to generalize from a small exploratory study as long as you state that this is your intention. Research students frequently try to make their findings apply to a wider world, as though doing so improves the value of their endeavours. Unfortunately, this is seldom true.

Case studies and generalization

Overall, generalization can be seen as a weak point in qualitative research: a case study is not a sample of one, it is not a sample at all (Bryman and Bell, 2003). The use of case studies and small samples in qualitative research makes it hard to make generalizations. This means either that external validity is not a problem with case studies because generalization is not an objective of qualitative research (Stake, 1978) or that the results may be generalizable (Schofield, 1990) through careful research design. It is certainly true that a lot of management research is based on in-depth case studies in a few companies, but the reality is that we simply don't know if success or disaster in one company is generalizable to others (Raimond, 1993). Many writers seem to agree that the findings of qualitative research can be generalized only to theory and not to populations. It is the quality of the theoretical inferences that makes qualitative research generalizable.

However, some authors make bolder claims. Yin suggests that replication of case study methods can achieve greater generalizability of theory (Yin, 2003), while Schofield (1990) argues that qualitative researchers can make informed judgements about the match between the single situation studied and others to which one might be interested in applying the concepts and conclusions of that study. This, she suggests, is what enables researchers to make informed judgements about where and to what extent they can generalize the results of their qualitative studies. She contends that careful selection of typical cases, or situations judged likely to become so in future, or those that are exceptional, can increase the generalizability of qualitative research. Gummeson (1991) goes even further by proposing that rich, deep data from a single case may enable generalization to other cases to be appropriate.

Unusually in management research literature, Raimond (1993) spends three chapters of his book on research design, considering the research validity, the reliability and the generalizability of the conclusions of three classics of business and management research. The studies he looks at are Peters and Waterman's (1982) *In Search of Excellence*, Michael Porter's (1971) industry analysis and his generic strategies, and Hofstede's (1984) *Culture's Consequences*. He takes the reader step by step through examining the premises of their arguments, their research designs and methods, the underlying logic of their argument, empirical tests of their reliability and generalizability and the conclusions they draw. There are useful additional lessons to be drawn from these studies, viewed in a historical perspective, as each is now at least 20 years old.

Additional tests of reliability and generalizability not found in the research methods literature reviewed above apply here in terms of the currency of the research and its applicability in different cultural contexts. For example, Peters and Waterman (1982) looked at 63 excellent companies and tried to ascertain what the lessons were that could be learnt from their success. By the mid 1980s, 14 of Peters and Waterman's companies were in trouble, but that may not diminish the range of lessons that can be learned from studying them and that will be applied elsewhere. The use of Hofstede's (1984) survey research in one organization (IBM) in the 1980s to make generalizations about the characteristics of national cultures today is also a key issue in terms of its generalizability and currency.

Alternative Criteria to Evaluate the Validity and Rigour of Research

Raimond (1993) suggests that there are limits to the uses of experimental and statistical research designs in management research, and that common sense and the use of a range of techniques, none of which is perfect in itself, could be the answer. It may be worth considering whether any of the established terms actually fit and can be used to measure the rigour of your research. He suggests some basic common sense tests:

- **Generalizability: Are the conclusions based on a wide enough range of cases and companies? Is the theory relevant only to the one company that you examined?**

- **Inter-subjectivity: It may be that this is the way you see it, but do others see it this way as well? Truth can be a shared delusion, but if others do share it, it builds credibility, so try it out on your peers – and your supervisor.**

- **Critical self-awareness: Are you fooling yourself? Team and group working can heighten critical self-awareness, but you also need to be able to identify what you have put in and to relate that to the outcomes.**

- **Repetition: Will it work again if it worked once already? Several books talk about the spiral of research, for example, Saunders et al., 2003 and Raimond, 1993, whereby data is collected to test theory, reflection on the data leads to amended theory, which is then tested and amended again.**

- **Verisimilitude: Try it out on other people and see if it rings true to them. Use colleagues, peers, teachers, friends to challenge your approach and ways of thinking.**

- **Theoretical congruence: What do others have to say about this issue?**

Lincoln and Guba (1985) suggest different but equally valuable criteria that could be used when evaluating qualitative research. These criteria were created out of unease with trying to apply measures that had originated from the more positivist quantitative disciplines and may be more suited to your research. Guba and Lincoln (1994) propose two different key criteria for assessing the reliability of qualitative research, which are trustworthiness and authenticity. Trustworthiness has four aspects in this scheme. The first is credibility – attested to by triangulation of the data collected, or by confirmation by those who were researched that the investigator correctly understood what was going on. The second is transferability – a key test here is whether the data is sufficiently rich to enable other researchers to make judgements about its possible transference to other contexts. Third, boosting the trustworthiness of qualitative research could be achieved by getting peers to audit your research process to confirm that it was carried out correctly – this is dependability. While this initially appears simpler to apply, it hinges on the systematic documentation of every part of the research process followed by extensive use of auditors to check the process. Finally, the auditing process may be carried further so that auditors can also check that personal or theoretical inclinations have not caused researchers to bias the research. This Guba and Lincoln (1994) describe as 'confirmability'.

Authenticity also has five criteria, according to Guba and Lincoln (1994), concerned with the wider context of the research. One is fairness – does it represent all viewpoints in a particular setting? Another is ontological authenticity – does the research help to enhance understanding of the social context? They also suggest three other aspects of authenticity which reflect their views as critical theorists – educative authenticity (has it helped people in the research to appreciate others' views in their setting?), catalytic authenticity (has it acted as an impetus to participants to change things?) and tactical authenticity (has it empowered them to do this?).

Common sense and the practicalities of doing research start to collide with some of these visions. Auditing a qualitative research study would be a massive undertaking given the quantities of data involved, and it would be difficult to guarantee the independence and rigour of the auditing process itself. For example, in order to guarantee impartiality should another institution do it, as with financial audits? Or even researchers from another discipline or research tradition? This is impractical advice for a postgraduate researcher working with limited resources.

Writing on ethnographic research, and so firmly in the qualitative camp, Hammersley (1992) takes a less extreme view and suggests that the plausibility and credibility of a researcher's claims are the key issues in qualitative research. Relevance is also crucially important, judged by an assessment of the importance of the topic within its field and what contribution it makes to the literature. This really brings us back to the need to make sound judgements about the reliability and significance of your research data, based on common sense and experience – something perhaps that many of us find hard to do when faced with new things.

Further Criteria to Consider: Bias, Samples and Currency

Depending on the subject of your research, there may be certain other aspects of the data that you are using that you need to pay attention to when trying to assess its reliability, validity and extent of generalization. Is there a bias in the academic articles you have collected? Much management literature and research is based on US data, or it may be Euro-centric or based on a few large companies. You need to think carefully about whether the material you have collected contains these biases and if so how might this affect your own research. If you are researching a small firm in Iceland and its market entry strategy when trying to enter the EU market, or part of it, how will journal articles about the market entry strategies of multinationals entering Asian markets add value to your work? You might be able to argue that small firms can learn from large firms, but you could also argue that what large firms do is not appropriate for small firms, which have greater resource constraints. In this example, cultural issues may also need to be taken into account, both the national culture and the internal business culture of the organization versus the ones cited in your academic and secondary sources.

The samples (or participants in more qualitative research) used for primary research within the business and management literature is also worth thinking about. A surprising amount of the research on consumer behaviour has been conducted using students as the sample, many of them MBA students or undergraduate business students. It is worth thinking about the extent to which this is representative of the population you might be interested in. A lot of the published academic work in the consumer behaviour literature on how people choose cars is actually based on studies of US college students, or people who work for particular US universities. Even if the participants are not all academics or students, it is worth considering the extent to which people living in university towns in America are typical of car buyers in other situations. Your study of price sensitivity in online purchasing is an interesting topic, but to undertake primary research using university students will limit the usefulness of the results, as students are not typical online purchasers.

Not only should you look for potential bias and the relevance of the samples used in your research and in published research, but in an ever faster-moving business environment, the currency of the journal articles and secondary sources needs consideration. While this should not prove a problem with your research, there have been instances where it has proved a handicap. One student who was working in a mobile phone shop to help pay for his studies was determined to base his dissertation around what he confidently predicted would be the failure of third-generation mobile technology to take off with customers in Oxford and hence the UK. All his initial interviews with customers, and his chats with his friends seemed to indicate that this was true. Unfortunately, once the products were available and the marketing was in full swing, a very different clientele arrived in his shop to buy the latest in electronic gadgetry, turning his theory on its head. He was left with the problem that he had collected his data too early, and had difficulty refocusing his research objectives.

When a paper or document was written may be important in determining its relevance to your research. Obviously there are some classic textbooks and journal articles that are still used and cited decades after their original publication, for example, Porter's *Competitive Strategy* in 1971 or Levitt's 'Marketing myopia' article, which was first published in *Harvard Business* Review in 1960. However, subject areas evolve, some more rapidly than others. The development and application of technology continues to impact and change functional business areas such as logistics, distribution, inventory control and even marketing communications, to name a few. As a result, material that was published three or four years ago may already be out of date and of limited value.

There is an additional problem in terms of the currency of research because academic research often takes a considerable time to conduct, analyse and write up. There then follows a lengthy review process before it is finally published. As a result, the research may be up to five years old before it is in the public domain (see Chapter 6). So your research may be much more current than the literature and this may be an issue that you will have to address. If you are researching the background to a very hot new topic in business, it may not have reached the academic journals. It is always worth asking the academic staff in your university or college if they go to academic conferences because often these topics are first debated in papers that you might find in the published proceedings of these conferences. Many also turn up on the Internet.

Checklist: Assessing the Rigour of the Research of Others

✓ Work out the key research questions that guided the research – do they reflect what you know about the world view of the researcher? What is the point of view of the researcher? Has the researcher explained his or her own values – does he or she demonstrate self-awareness?

✓ Is the study quantitative or qualitative? Where was it carried out? When was it carried out?

✓ If quantitative, what is the sample size, how was the sample selected, was the appropriate statistical analysis used?

✓ If testing a theory, could it work with the worst case? Or are the cases used chosen to demonstrate the theory in action?

✓ Has the theory been tested against an exhaustive and extensive range of examples? Or were the ones used chosen just to support the author's ideas?

✓ Is it internally logical and consistent? Do the parts fit together?

✓ What tests of inter-subjectivity and theoretical congruence has the author used? i.e did the author peer review the methodology? What do others have to say about this issue? (Is there a good review of literature on the subject?)

✓ What was the context in which the research was carried out – cultural, political and social?

✓ How does the author arrive at the 'why' questions? (Why does it happen this way, etc.)

✓ Is the analytical framework or construct used here based on data from other studies? (Theoretical congruence.)

✓ What is its range of coverage? What does it not cover?

✓ Does it match with your own experience? Does it help explain other examples or cases you are familiar with? (inter-subjectivity tests.)

Checklist: Assessing Your Own Research

✓ Did I actually research what I said I would in the title and research objectives?

✓ How rigorous was my data collection?

✓ Is there bias either in my assumptions or in the design of the research or in the data collected?

✓ Did I use more than one method of data collection?

✓ Were my methods appropriate for the topic?

✓ Have I really provided a clear and logical blueprint of how I went about my research so that someone else could replicate it?

✓ If I only gather information from a small number of people, to what extent can I generalize my findings to a whole sector or country or management theme?

✓ Should I be trying to generalize at all?

✓ If using a case study approach, what is the case about?

✓ Have I used multiple sources of evidence?

✓ How would I do it differently if I were to conduct the research again?

Summary

This chapter has attempted to clarify the complex concepts of validity, reliability and generalization. It has outlined the ongoing academic debate about whether or not generalization is possible or even desirable. The chapter has also provided checklists to help you in assessing the rigour of the research of others that you read and may wish to use and of your own research.

Suggested Activity

Read the précis of a piece of research by Martin and Bush (2000) in the box below and apply the principles of validity, reliability and generalization that you have learned from this chapter. Ask yourself the following questions:

1   How valid is this research?
2   How reliable is this research?
3   To what extent were the results generalized and to what extent should the results have been generalized?

(Suggested answers are given below.)

- Research title – Do role models influence teenagers' purchase intentions and behaviour?
- Stated research objective is to find out which individual or group of individuals has the strongest influence on adolescent consumer purchase intention and behaviour.
- Sample base – USA high school students aged 13–18 years, from 74 schools in one metropolitan area.
- Convenience sample of 218 questionnaires completed in front of the interviewer.
- Used a five-item scale on role model influence and an eleven-item scale on purchase intention adapted from other cited authors.
- Basic demographic questions asked of sample.
- Main findings – parents are most important influencers on teenagers' consumption patterns; Caucasian teenagers perceive fathers as role models more than African-American teenagers do.

Suggested answers

1. Is it valid?

It is of questionable internal validity (see pages 126–28) because the research objective is to explore both purchase intentions and behaviour, and the research findings focus on who the important influencers are but do not distinguish between purchase intention and purchase behaviour.

Also scales have been borrowed from other authors without questioning their rigour and relevance to this particular study.

2. Is it reliable?

The size and composition of the sample and of those who actually responded – high school students selected from urban areas in one US city on a convenience basis – means that you cannot draw reliable conclusions that apply to any other group of people. Only one method of data collection has been used and completing questionnaires in front of the interviewer can introduce bias. The measures that have been used are not reliable (see page 129), and there is a lack of triangulation (see page 131).

(Continued)

(Continued)

3. To what extent were the results generalised and to what extent should the results be generalised?

This study uses only American secondary school students from one urban area and then draws conclusions about the attitudes of teenagers towards influences and role models. The research concludes that Caucasian teenagers perceive fathers as role models more than African American teenagers do – this is too large a generalization to make from this very narrow study and goes outside the stated research boundaries.

Discussion Questions

1   What is your considered view on generalization in management research?

2   How can you improve the validity of your own research?

Further Reading

Raimond, P. (1993) *Management Projects: Design, Research and Presentation.* **London: Chapman and Hall.** The strength of this text lies in the discussion of three leading studies in business research and the dissection of validity, reliability and generalization of each. This is well worth reading if you can get access to a copy.

10 Writing Up and Beyond

How Do I Present my Research?

The aim of this chapter is to give you the confidence to get started on the process of describing and presenting your research. Many researchers feel quite confused and may even start to panic or try to put off as long as possible the moment when they must start to write up their dissertation. Sadly, there is much high-quality research that is overlooked because of the way in which it was written up. This chapter begins by helping you to identify who your audience are and then goes on to provide a guide to how to plan and present your work in order to show it off to its best advantage.

Who Are my Audience?

Think carefully about the audience for your piece of work and whom you are writing it for. Who will read it and who are the most important readers from your point of view? Your partner or immediate family may have a look at it to please you, but they are not your audience (and in our experience they rarely read the whole thing). Potential employers are another possibility, but they are unlikely to look beyond the abstract or executive summary, and neither will the people who participated in your research and to whom you promised to show the dissertation. Some of our students are sponsored by family businesses or by their employers. Naturally, they want to produce something that will be useful to the sponsoring organization. They carry out a piece of research that borders on consultancy and then try to write it up as such for their dissertation. Similarly, our MBA or DMS dissertation students and sometimes those doing an MSc in International Business or Management may think that they are writing a report as a piece of consultancy for the organization they have studied or had access to. Unfortunately, you cannot do this satisfactorily and also meet the academic requirements at Masters' level, and it is not possible to please two very separate audiences with one document.

If you are asked to write a consultancy report for an organization, you should produce something that is wholly different from an academic dissertation. For a start, it will be much shorter, it may well be in the form of a presentation with a brief supporting document and is very unlikely to be concerned with academic references, in depth description of the research methods undertaken, a critical review of the literature or a reflection on the research process, all of which you will certainly need for your dissertation. A consultancy report will probably focus on an analysis of the problem or problems found in the area studied and a series of recommendations as to how these could be tackled over a particular timescale, with an assessment of the costs and benefits of various courses of action. If you need to produce a report for an organization, perhaps as a condition for being granted access to the organization in the first place or to satisfy them that they have sponsored you wisely, then it is very important that you agree with them at the outset the precise purpose and nature of the report that they are going to receive. You must expect to write two different documents to satisfy your very different audiences, and you should bear this in mind when planning your writing time.

Your key audience will be your supervisor, who may or may not be the first marker for your dissertation, and the dissertation second marker, an independent person whom you are unlikely to meet. It is likely that it will be marked by at least two academics. It is important to note that you are not just writing for your supervisor, who by now you should know well, but also for complete strangers, who do not know you and may not be experts in your specific topic. You must not assume that whoever reads your work already knows how much effort and how much hard work you have put in to it, or has looked at earlier drafts. The markers can only mark the final dissertation, regardless of whether an earlier version was better. They will probably read it only once, so the clarity of your writing and the logical structure of your work are absolutely vital to these strangers if they are to follow and understand your research. Most institutions also have external examiners or third markers who read a sample of dissertations to check that they meet nationally recognized guidelines for what constitutes a Masters' dissertation, but they are there for quality control purposes and will not normally change your marks. Realistically, these markers may be the only people who ever read your dissertation cover to cover, apart from yourself. They constitute your key audience and it is they whom you must impress in order to get good marks.

Your university will have explicit rules and regulations about the format and length of your Masters' dissertation. It is vital that you read the guides that are given to you and that you follow the rules closely. If you deviate from them and produce a 'different' dissertation, it will be at your peril. Unfortunately, presenting your dissertation in a 'creative' manner may well mean that you fail. Few institutions will allow you much latitude. A student of ours proposed writing up his MBA business dissertation in the form of a stage play. Having recovered from our surprise, we strongly urged him to rethink his 'creativity' and fortunately he did. During your studies, you should have been given documentation that contains the specific requirements of your examining institution. By the time you come to write up your research, it may well have been many months since you looked at it – and you may have lost it altogether. Before you start to write is the time to retrieve this documentation and to study it carefully. However good a piece of research yours is, if it does not fulfil those requirements, it will not pass. Examiners expect to see dissertations in a certain style, so make life easier for yourself and go along with these requirements even if you privately do not agree with them. You can argue once you have the qualification.

Your university or college will also have explicit marking criteria for your dissertation that you should look at closely. If it has not been included in your course documentation, you should ask your supervisor or course manager for a copy, as you are entitled to have this information. As you write up your dissertation you should ensure that every marking criterion in the course documents is met to the best of your ability. For example, if one of the criteria is 'demonstrates the ability to integrate theory with practice and to synthesize an argument', you need to double check that you have linked theory derived from the academic literature to any primary research you might have carried out. You then also need to produce an 'informed' opinion in order to meet that particular criterion. Your opinion, of course, needs to be informed by the academic research you have carried out. It is vital that, when you have started to write up your dissertation, you regularly go through every section, checking that you have covered the aspects that the markers are going to look for. It is surprising how often Masters' students miss out key aspects that are clearly stated on the marking criteria. Marks cannot be given for evidence that is not there.

As well as explicit criteria and requirements, there may also be a particular implicit culture or preference in a department or among a set of supervisors regarding the presentation and style of a dissertation. You should try to pick up on these. Pay particular attention in classes devoted to 'writing up' for hints on good practice. Look at previous recent dissertations in your college or university library that have attracted good marks. Find out who the supervisors were – this is often shown in the acknowledgements near the front – and ask the supervisor if they can remember what it was about the dissertation that was particularly striking. Many markers have particular preferences and if you can ascertain what these are and pander to them, then so much the better. Even issues of style may count. For example, some markers prefer tables and graphs to be in the main body of the text, while others prefer them as appendices. Ask your supervisor which he or she prefers. There may be a recommended style of writing that you should find out about, such as only using the third person, or avoiding a journalistic style. It is important that you get this right.

Planning your Dissertation

Before you can start to write anything, you need to read through all your notes and to construct a detailed plan of your dissertation, which you should discuss with your supervisor. Your dissertation plan will be quite different from the research proposal you probably wrote at the start of your research for your dissertation. This should be as detailed as you can make it with a logical development of your thinking and a clear structure that you can work to. It is worth spending several days just reading through your notes and wrestling with your plan, as the very act of planning your dissertation will enable you to start the thought processes needed to analyse what you have read and to write effectively.

It is important, however, that you do start to write. Many textbooks point out that writing helps to clarify your thinking and if you are in a muddle about some key aspect, it may well be very helpful to sit down and write about it, even if you end up by not using a lot of what you have written in the first place. Once you start to write, you may end up revising your plan – do not worry; this is a working document that is bound to be subject to some quite substantial changes as you go along.

Some students worry about the order in which they should be writing things. If you are very worried about writing and lack confidence that you have the right style, you could start with something that is relatively straightforward such as the methods chapter (see the suggested structure below) and get feedback from your supervisor early on. Otherwise, we would suggest that you start with the chapters on which you need to spend the most time – these are usually the literature review and analysis chapters (see the section on structure later in this chapter). These are also the most difficult chapters to get right and you will need to revise them several times as you go along. Whatever you do, do not leave the analysis chapter until the end so that it becomes a rush job – it is much too important. Some students start with the introduction while many others write it last.

Writing in English

It may be that you are writing a dissertation in your second or third language. You will need to find out from your institution what their requirements are in regard to the level of written English. Many universities have departments that will help students with their academic writing in order to improve the clarity, but they will not write your dissertation for you. There are also professional proofreading services available that charge by the hour. In our experience, it is better to try to express an idea simply and clearly than use terminology that you are unsure of. Minor lapses in how you express yourself grammatically are generally accepted by supervisors and examiners. However, if the reader can not make sense of the point you are trying to convey then you will not convince them that you know your subject and will be likely therefore to fail. Generally speaking, supervisors will not correct your English grammer or syntax, so if you think you will need help, ask for it early on in your research. Asking other students to read and correct your work may not prove as helpful as you imagine.

Presenting an effective argument

Your dissertation should be an effective piece of writing and in order to do that it should tell a 'story' that has a beginning, a middle and an end. The reader should be able to follow a case or argument that gradually builds up throughout the dissertation. This means that you need to have a really clear idea of what your case or theme is and that you need to be able to argue it. If you analyse the writings of academics in the social sciences, including business, it is clear that they do more than just report their research findings; they are trying to persuade you that their approach is the one to follow. No one starts from the viewpoint of not having a position, or of being completely objective. You need to be able to persuade your readers that what you have found in your research is significant and that your conclusions really do stack up.

In order to be persuasive in your dissertation, you need to be able to write in a clear and consistent style, that reveals how your key points are developed throughout the dissertation. There are a number of formal ways of constructing arguments and two useful chapters on this can be found in Bryman and Bell (2003) and Fisher (2004). Other research methods textbooks such as Saunders et al., 2003 and Collis and Hussey, 2003 also contain helpful chapters on writing styles and presenting your research.

Constructing an argument in a dissertation is likely to be rather different from how you might approach an argument that you are putting forward in a discussion with friends. If you sat down to debate a topical issue, for example, you would probably start by stating your position or opinion. You might then go on to try and support your point of view by marshalling some evidence in its favour – something you read or saw on television, perhaps. In a written argument, you would probably approach it the other way round, by laying out the evidence first and then suggesting that it supports a key opinion or conclusion.

In your dissertation, once you have told everyone what it is that you are intending to do and how you will do it (your introduction and methods chapters – see the section on structure later), you need to construct an argument based around a number of key themes that will run through the rest of your dissertation. Each piece of evidence that you produce – whether from your literature review, your analysis of secondary data or your primary data collection – will make a point about something that is related to one of your research objectives or questions. Each point that you make may be supported or contradicted by other evidence that you need to discuss and explain, and perhaps develop further. Eventually, you will make a judgement, because by this stage your opinion is valuable and highly informed by all the work you have been doing, and decide that there are certain key points that will form the basis of your conclusions, and you will then discuss the implications for theory and practice of these key points.

You can view the process of constructing arguments as consisting of a number of stages, as shown below. In our experience, everyone always gets to stage 1, but it is vitally important is that you get well beyond stage 1, or your dissertation is unlikely to pass.

Stages in Constructing an Argument in a Dissertation

- **Stage 1: describe what people have said – evidence from the literature review, secondary and primary data collection.**

- **Stage 2: your evaluation of all that evidence – is it valid, how reliable, how significant?**

- **Stage 3: apply the evidence to the context you are looking at – does it fit, can you provide possible explanations?**

- **Stage 4: make generalizations – to other possible contexts, to management theory. Conclude whether you think it stands up.**

Fisher (2004) describes a number of different approaches to constructing an argument. One is to use a dialectical approach, as originally proposed by Hegel, nearly 200 years ago. Hegel suggested that arguments took the form of a proposition or thesis, a contradiction of that proposition or antithesis, and then a synthesis of these ideas which moved the argument forward to a higher level, where the synthesis then became a proposition to which an antithesis was proposed – and so the whole cycle continued. A dialectical argument as applied to business and management might be to propose a thesis or formal idea, for example, that a certain new management practice is a good thing. The practical realities that might undermine this idea could be seen to be the antithesis, everyday life and the involvement of people, and, in this example, resistance to change. The next stage is a synthesis, where understanding of the idea grows so that there is a higher level of shared knowledge and the contradictions are less important (Fisher, 2004). This becomes the next thesis and so the cycle continues. Fisher suggests that the dialectic can provide an alternative form of argument that could be used very effectively in a dissertation. Unfortunately, we have never seen this attempted in practice, but it could be a useful way of writing up an action research project, where the staged model described above is likely to be much less helpful.

Another approach is to follow the classic model adopted by many business and management academics in published articles based on quantitative research. These articles tend to follow the same pattern: an introduction, a section setting out a theory and hypotheses, a discussion of the methods used to test the hypotheses, a report on the results and a discussion of their implications. Bryman and Bell describe one such article and analyse the way the argument has been constructed. They then look at an example of a journal article based on qualitative research and find that the structure is very similar, with a review of the literature substituted for the hypotheses section (Bryman and Bell, 2003). This type of structure is the one frequently suggested for management and business dissertations, and is similar to the structure of the overall report that we suggest later in the chapter. However, it can be very rigid, particularly in the journal format used by many mainstream management journals. It is also important to remember that Masters' dissertations are usually 15000 to 20000 words long, while these journal articles are much shorter – only 5000 to 7000 words. In our view, in a document that is at least three times the length of an average academic journal article, you cannot afford to leave all the stage 2, 3 and 4 levels of your argument until one chapter near the end. We encourage our students to engage with the higher stage 2, 3 and 4 levels of argument throughout the literature review and findings chapters (see the section on structure later in the chapter) so that when they get to the conclusions, there is a drawing together of arguments that have already been raised and rehearsed. If you have 20000 words, you have the luxury of being able to recapitulate and re-emphasize themes that have previously been discussed and developed – if you have only 6000 words, you do not. Remember your readers – over the course of 20000 words that may well not be read all at one sitting, they will need gentle reminders of key findings and key themes introduced earlier in your dissertation.

Critical Writing

When you come to write your literature review as part of your dissertation, you will be expected to 'critically engage with the literature'. It is worth thinking for a moment about what this actually means. There is a reasonable amount of published work on the subject of writing a good literature review. Saunders et al. (2003) and most other business research methods textbooks have a chapter on 'critically reviewing the literature'. Hart (1998) devotes a whole book to the subject, but his description of the purpose of a literature review omits much reference to the critical reflective element, as do the other authors cited. Hart suggests that the literature review must be used to justify the topic and that a key objective is to provide a clear and balanced picture of current leading concepts, theories and data relevant to the topic of study. Its purpose is also to provide a methodological rationalization for the primary research. As such it should incorporate a description of previous work on the topic, of what you find wrong in that work and a proposal for action to fill the gap or solve the problem and an explanation of its benefits. Late in the book (p. 176), Hart has a section in which he attempts to define effective criticism and later still, when discussing the writing up of the review, he suggests that three blocks of work should be considered. These are a summary of existing work on the subject, a critical evaluation of previous work and some conclusions about the work done to date on the topic. Hart assumes that the literature review is a preface to carrying out some primary research, though in fact at Masters' level this is often not the case.

It is worth thinking about what the examiners – the people who will be reading your dissertation – will be looking for. When we ask people to 'engage with the literature' while writing a dissertation, we are asking them to read and understand it, and also to appraise it and to assess its worth and its utility to the central research question or inquiry in the dissertation. We know that your examiners will want to see evidence of a wide range of reading and of an up to date and coherent knowledge of the literature. In this chapter, we have also discussed how you might go about analysing argument and appraising what you read. We have come to the conclusion that the reason we have struggled to teach students to understand what constitutes a good critical literature review is that we all have real problems with the word 'critical'. Our advice is to banish thoughts of criticism and to focus on a process of appraisal. Your examiners will also be looking for an ability to synthesize – to bring together evidence from different places and to weave it into a constructive and coherent theme.

There are a number of ways in which you can structure your writing so that you develop your argument in a way that is clear to your examiners. It is worth spending quite a lot of time before and as you start to write on designing the structure of your literature review, as re-structuring it later, while not impossible, can be quite difficult. Show early drafts to your supervisor if that is possible, because advice at an early stage can be very helpful. There is no correct structure; below we suggest six possible structures, which we have described as the classic funnel, the inverted funnel, the lonesome pine, the timeline, combining concepts and linked themes. It may be helpful to you when you are drafting your literature review to try jotting down your main headings using each of these suggestions, so that you can pick one that suits your material – or invent one of your own.

The classic funnel

Many literature reviews start by describing a number of fairly broad general themes that have been traced in the literature, using references to lots of authors and covering a fairly wide range of topics. Using the classic funnel structure, these literature reviews gradually narrow down the range of discussion to focus on one or two clear themes that relate back, as the funnel broadens slightly towards the bottom, to one or more of the research questions or objectives set for the dissertation (see Figure 10.1). This classic structure can be extremely effective.

The inverted funnel

It is possible, and may indeed be desirable, to write your literature review in the opposite way to the one described above so that it has a structure of an inverted funnel. You

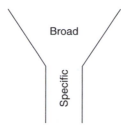

Figure 10.1   Classic funnel

could start it with a very narrow focus or theme and then broaden the discussion to bring in further authors and linked topics (see Figure 10.2). For example, a literature review that began by discussing the impact of parent–child interaction on purchasing decisions in the consumer behaviour literature could broaden out into a review of authors drawn from the sociology and psychology literature on the changing role of children in the family.

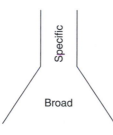

Figure 10.2   Inverted funnel

The line of argument tree

Another useful structure for your literature review is to think of it as resembling a solitary tree. The core or trunk runs right through the piece and is a unifying line of argument that you are using, or possibly a core central theme. The main branches should then consist of each supporting piece of major literature that provides evidence to support the core line of argument. Subsidiary pieces of evidence then serve to form additional twigs and leaves or pine needles on each branch (see Figure 10.3).

The timeline

It may be that your literature review will track the chronological development of an idea and or its impact in practice. In that case, your structure will be close to a timeline

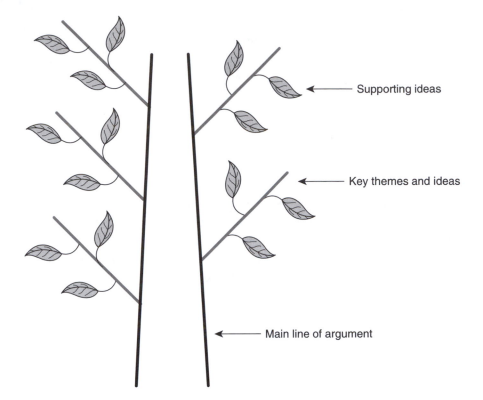

Figure 10.3   Main line of argument tree

as key dates of publication or indications of adoption of the idea or practice will have a major significance (see Figure 10.4). One recent literature review that we saw tracked the development of ideas about how innovations are taken up and diffused. Because one author in particular had dominated this field over a long period, a timeline approach was a very useful means of tracking the diffusion of thinking about the diffusion of innovation and assessing its impact and relevance to the dissertation objectives.

1998   2005

Figure 10.4   Horizontal timeline

Combining concepts

A business dissertation can and should look beyond the immediate boundaries of the business literature. You may find relevant discussions and concepts when reading other

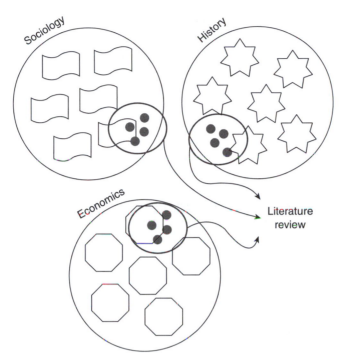

Figure 10.5   Distinct patterns combining to form a single literature review

subjects. You should attempt to integrate and combine these concepts in your literature review (see Figure 10.5).

Linked themes

Another possible structure for your literature review is to think of it as consisting of a number of themes of roughly equal weight which are linked to each other as in a chain. Together these links form a strong and cohesive structure (see Figure 10.6).

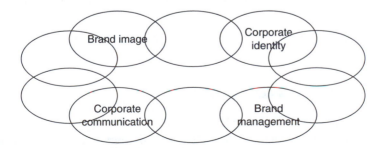

Figure 10.6   Linked themes

Vivas and Presentations

This chapter makes the assumption that your dissertation will be assessed in written form, but it is possible that your institution will ask you to give a presentation of your results or will invite you to a formal viva or discussion of what you have done. You need to check with your institution what the norm is; some universities ask postgraduate research students to present their research proposals or a progress report, or give a full-blown presentation of the key findings. If this is the case, then make sure your presentation materials cover what is required and that the core information is clearly and simply communicated, practise your presentation and time yourself. If possible, get a mock panel of would-be examiners together (from other people on your course perhaps) and get them to ask you questions. You must be able to defend your research topic, design and the subsequent findings.

Structure of your Dissertation

Although there is no one 'correct' way to structure your dissertation, there are certain features that the markers would expect to see as distinct sections or chapters within your work. You may find that you end up with a dissertation that has seven to 10 chapters overall. Again, your dissertation guide or course documents and your supervisor will provide advice as to the structure they expect, which you should follow. An MBA or DMS dissertation may have a slightly different emphasis from an MA or MSc, as there is likely to be a stronger focus on practical problem-solving. This may mean that it has slightly different sections or chapters. Within the dissertation, each chapter should also have a consistent structure. It should contain a brief introduction that sets out its purpose and introduces the subject matter; the main section, which may be further subdivided into subsections, each dealing with a discrete topic; and then a brief summary of what has been said in the chapter, what it contributes to the overall aim of the dissertation and, ideally, a link in to the next chapter. You could imagine each chapter to be a sandwich, the introduction and summary are the slices of bread holding the sandwich together and the filling is the interesting discussion part in the middle, but you need all the ingredients to make a complete sandwich, and a full set of sandwiches to make a dissertation!

Most Masters' dissertations should normally contain the elements described below.

Abstract/executive summary

An abstract needs to be approximately 300 words (the dissertation regulations will normally specify the word length) and it should be separate from the main body of the work, on its own page. In many dissertations, the abstract is not included in the word count and the page containing the abstract is not numbered in the same way as the bulk of the text. For example, the abstract, acknowledgements and contents pages are sometimes numbered using the Roman system of numerals, with Arabic numerals reserved for the rest, so that Chapter 1 of the main dissertation text starts on page 1. Again, your course guide may be very specific as to how you number pages and you must follow this. The abstract should try to be a bird's eye view of the whole dissertation. It should include the aim of the dissertation, an outline of the research methods undertaken and a brief summary of the key findings. An abstract does not normally include references. It can be helpful to think of this short piece as a selling tool to encourage the reader to read the entire piece of research. If you are doing a DMS or MBA dissertation, you may well be expected to include an executive summary instead of an abstract. An executive summary, if it is required, is usually longer than an abstract. It should state the purpose of the work, how it was carried out, the key results and the main recommendations or implications that arise from the findings. It should be written in formal business English, as though for a busy senior manager who may not have time to read the entire document. You may find it useful to write an executive summary for your own use, which you can use later to submit with job applications.

Introduction

The introduction should set the context of the whole dissertation. You should be able to justify why this topic is worth researching and writing about both in academic and business terms. For example, if your dissertation topic were on the implications of globalization on promotional material in a fast-moving consumer goods sector, then you would need to explain why globalization was worth researching as an academic subject and also why this subject mattered to businesses. Your introduction should be able to set the scene rather like the opening of a play, so that your audience has a clear mental picture of what you are trying to achieve. You can also be explicit in stating what you will not be including. At Masters' level, you should allow yourself to be selective and set your parameters firmly early on. Many topics overlap, but you should be clear in defining the area you will focus on and the areas you will be excluding.

You will need to set out your specific objectives and research questions, or possibly hypotheses, which you will attempt to answer in the course of your dissertation. The reader needs to know *what* you are trying to find out. Sometimes it is helpful to include these in the introduction as a bulleted list. Objectives, research questions and hypotheses take time to think about and need careful phrasing in order to make them achievable (see Chapters 2 and 3). You will definitely need to return to them at the end of your dissertation to show to what extent you have achieved them. Occasionally when you are writing up your research, you may find that you have answered a rather different set of research questions or fulfilled slightly different research objectives from those you originally proposed. It is important to be internally consistent. If this happens, you may need to alter the original research objectives and questions slightly to bring them in to line with what you actually did. An introduction should also mention what the expected outcome of your research project will be. Examples might be adding to the body of knowledge in this subject area, the testing of a particular theory, or the creation of a conceptual framework that could be tested at a later date.

Your introduction should also describe the structure of the rest of the dissertation so the reader knows what to expect. Try not to let this become rather mechanistic, Chapter 1 is about … Chapter 2 focuses on … Chapter 3 outlines … and so on. It should demonstrate that you have a logical and considered approach to the topic, which the markers will appreciate.

Background, country or sector information (optional)

Certain types of dissertation lend themselves to having a separate chapter that outlines recent activity in a business sector, for example mergers and acquisitions in the pharmaceutical industry, or a largely descriptive account of a country market or industrial sector. This can assist the reader in understanding quite complex business trends, cultural issues important to a particular context or an unusual industry background and gives a foundation for the rest of the dissertation. Relevant country, trade, sector and financial secondary source material can be used in this type of chapter. It is important not to make it too long, as the purpose of this chapter is to get the reader up to speed on the key issues that underpin the discussion in the rest of the dissertation. Nor should it be too general – long descriptions of the geography of China are not needed. If you are in doubt as to whether you need this section at all, you can probably cut it out. A useful example of a background chapter was in a recent MBA dissertation that was looking at the business case for investing in solar power in the UK. The dissertation included a succinct background chapter on the evidence for climate change, recent government energy policy and the development of renewable energy as an alternative source of power. This was important in helping the reader to understand the nature of the business case for solar energy. Some dissertations incorporate a background section within the introduction chapter, but it may be worthwhile creating a separate chapter for the information, depending on its length and complexity.

Literature review

The literature review is a critical component of your Masters' dissertation. It is the core component of the academic part of the Masters' dissertation. Some MA and MSc dissertations are based only on secondary data, without any primary research, and in these courses the literature review may account for up to 80 percent of the dissertation. For other Masters' courses, the literature review is still likely to be at least half the dissertation, while for MBA and DMS students, the literature review may take up around 40 percent of the word limit.

The literature review is your opportunity to demonstrate to the reader how much you know and at what depth about your chosen topic's literature. You will be expected to know the work of the leading authors in the subject area and to be able to integrate their main concepts into your own argument. At Masters' level, it is not enough to produce a 'shopping list' of what certain authors have published without any critical thought and discussion. You need to be able to extract key themes that are relevant to your research objectives or questions and to be able to assess the research you have read about for its validity, reliability and significance and relevance to your objectives. See Chapters 7 and 9 for more on this.

When you are writing your literature review, you can start by deciding on one or two key themes that you want to explore that are relevant to your research topic. Some students choose to start with a broad theme and then gradually narrow it down until they end up with a highly focused discussion on one particular aspect. Other students do the reverse and start with a narrow focus and then broaden out their discussion. For example, if you were interested in how people make choices between brands, a literature review could begin with a wide discussion of the literature on consumer decision-making processes. It could then explore some of the key influences on individual decision-making and move on to focus on the role of children and their influence on the decision-making process. It could then go even further and narrow down to a particular type of product purchase in a particular context.

It is important always to remember when writing that the person who is going to mark your dissertation is probably only going to read it once. It is therefore a good idea to make it as easy to read as possible. Do not adopt a deliberately obscure style in the hope that it makes you sound 'more academic' – the best written articles are the ones that are easy to read and yet contain some challenging ideas. This is what you should be trying to aim for and the literature review chapter or chapters should give you the opportunity to do this. Do include plenty of 'signposts' in your writing. It is really important to tell your readers what you are going to discuss in one section and what is coming up in the next. While the logic of your thoughts may seem obvious, it may not be as obvious to them as it seems to you. At the end of your literature review it is again helpful to the reader to have a short summary of the key discussion points that you are going to carry forward for further exploration later on, perhaps in your primary research or in the analysis chapter.

It can be all too easy to lose your focus when you are trying to write your literature review. If you think you may be wandering away from your chosen topic area, go back to your working title and objectives and assess where, if at all, the section of the literature review that you are currently writing fits in. If you can see no real connection and couldn't justify the section to your supervisor then stop, put it to one side or in a separate file on the computer, and begin again with a different section. If you notice that you do have a tendency to wander off the track, it may help to attach your key research objectives on a piece of paper to the top of your computer screen. That way you really have little excuse for not checking regularly that you have stayed on your chosen path.

The literature review will take time to write and many researchers find it the hardest part of the dissertation to put together. Many textbook authors (e.g. see Saunders et al., 2003: 45) suggest that it is something that you will start to write early on in the dissertation, and that you will then continue to add to it and to refine it right up until you hand in your dissertation. This can seem a truly daunting prospect! We suggest that it may take several attempts before you feel ready to show even a part of your literature review to your supervisor for comment. Do not be disheartened, the threading together of your own argument from the work of many other authors and academic sources is complicated and demanding.

Methods

For some reason, this chapter often causes confusion among Masters' students and is therefore frequently given minimal attention. Students tend to leave it to the end to write and it becomes a bit of a rushed job. Some of the methods chapters we see are very short indeed. This is a great pity, because the methods chapter can really give you the opportunity to show how good a researcher you are and it is not difficult to do it well, if you leave yourself sufficient time. Your markers will be interested in the process of your research as well as the outcome and it is in this chapter that you lay down the processes and procedures you used to find out the answers to your research objectives, questions or hypotheses.

It is in the methods chapter that you will describe, using the appropriate research methods vocabulary, your overall approach to your research. Drawing on the fairly extensive literature on research methods, your chapter will include a discussion about whether you are following an inductive or deductive approach, or a mixture of the two, and why your choice of approach is appropriate for your dissertation topic. At postgraduate level, some reflection on your own potential for bias and your own internal 'world view' is important (see Chapter 8). We all hold certain beliefs, preconceptions and values that can influence our research. You need to demonstrate a level of self-understanding before you begin to describe and justify the research methods and data collection tools you have used.

Even if you have chosen to pursue a dissertation that has been based on secondary sources alone, you will still need to write up a methods section in your dissertation. This will include a justification for the choice of the topic and the significance of the literature, a discussion of your basic research philosophy and a description of how you selected and collated the literature to be included in your review. Other methods chapters should include a strong justification of why you chose certain data collection tools, such as why you chose to carry out in-depth interviews with a small number of key informants rather than send questionnaires to many more, or why structured observation was a useful tool when combined with self-completion questionnaires. You should draw on the main research methods books and journal articles when you are discussing your data collection methods. Ideally, you should aim to use more than one data collection method and/or different types of data sources in order to strengthen your findings (known as triangulation, see Chapter 9). Some researchers find it helpful to create flowcharts or diagrams of their research process and how their data collection methods fit together. You can include these in the methods chapter as an aid to the reader, but try to construct your own diagram if you are going to do this – or at the very least adapt one, giving due acknowledgement to the originator, from one of the textbooks.

Your methods chapter should also include a discussion of any difficulties you have encountered in the collection or processing of your data. If achieving your target number of completed questionnaires proved difficult or impossible, this should be mentioned and you should make an appraisal of the impact this might have had on the validity of the outcome. Many students use part of the methods chapter as an opportunity to reflect on their whole approach, along the lines of: 'if I were to do this again I would do x or y differently'. This could consist of anything from better time management, the use of different data collection tools, the asking of different interview questions or the use of different companies as case studies. Once again, you can use this as an opportunity – even if it has all gone very differently from how you had intended – to show that you have a thoughtful and considered approach to doing research. Your markers will be trying to assess how rigorous, valid and reliable your research process and output has been, and so you need to be explicit about what you did and why you did it, and what you learned from the process. Extracts from a researcher's diary or a piece of reflective writing (see Chapter 8) may fit in well here. An honest approach to the limitations of your research will gain you more respect and probably higher marks than ignoring or hiding problems when you are writing it up.

This honesty should also be applied to your first attempts at data analysis. Towards the end of your methods chapter, you should discuss how you propose to analyse the data or the literature. Will you use your stated research objectives as the basis for your analysis? Will you use some key themes from your literature review as the basis for the analysis of the primary data you collect? Will you use the key ideas that were mentioned by your interviewees as the basis for your analysis? Will you try to use content analysis and why? Are you going to run some statistical tests to test your hypotheses and why might you use those particular tests? Your data may prove quite difficult to analyse. Many researchers find that they do not manage a perfect analysis of their data at their first attempt. You may find yourself trying several different types of analysis. You should be prepared to write these up in your methods chapter, as it will demonstrate the level of serious thought and endeavour that has gone into producing your rigorous results, even if some of the early attempts at data analysis were not successful.

Findings, analysis and discussion

Depending on your chosen topic and the expectations of your examining institution, findings, analysis and discussion may be split into discrete chapters. Some universities and examiners may wish to see a chapter that is devoted exclusively to your findings or results. The findings of your research are purely that; they describe what you found in your research, such as who said what at interviews or the statistical output from testing a hypothesis in a particular way. You might use one of the graphics packages or SPSS or Microsoft Excel to generate charts, graphs and tables that present this information. What is crucial at this point is that you do not mistake description of your findings for an analysis of their meaning and that you do not present tables and diagrams without any explanation of their significance, relevance to your objectives and authority. One of us tries to steer her students away from even writing a chapter headed 'findings', as she finds that it so often tends to be mistaken by students for analysis. The resulting text is no more than a gentle children's story, with lots of description but nothing more substantial.

What is important, assuming that you have carried out some primary research, is that you do make the most of the data you have collected. One of us has seen too many dissertations when the actual 'findings' are buried in tables in appendices and never properly discussed – this is a terrible waste when you think how much effort you have to put in to collect primary data in the first place. So your results were not as original, far-ranging or conclusive as you expected? Don't worry, they very seldom are. We all start our research with high hopes and expectations, but the practical realities of carrying out research in the field mean that we may end up with something that is much less startling, but nevertheless has a modest contribution to make to knowledge about the subject. You should celebrate your achievement in carrying it through and make the most of it, while being realistic about its significance.

Whether you have a separate 'findings' chapter or not, your chapter in which you report on the analysis of your results and your discussion must use evidence that is actually based on your analysis of the relevant literature and/or the primary research from which you draw your key conclusions. Our view is that the analysis and discussion belong together, as analysis of your findings should be the prerequisite for a discussion of their implications. As examiners, we have both come across examples of Masters' dissertations where the discussion was based purely on the author's opinion, rather than on any analysis of what he or she had read or found out. It can almost be as if the discussion had been written before doing any research and had been not changed by it afterwards. The main purpose of this chapter or chapters of your dissertation is to pull together and to integrate theories derived from the academic literature with the findings of the research you have undertaken, and to discuss your informed opinion and ideas based on the evidence you have presented. Whether it is an MA, MSc, MBA or DMS dissertation, the analysis and discussion will form a significant portion of your dissertation. With the literature review, it will take the longest time to think about and write up, so you will need to try to plan for this.

Recommendations or implications (optional)

A chapter that deals with the recommendations or implications of your analysis is particularly relevant if you are doing an MBA or a DMS dissertation. You might be able to make specific, actionable recommendations for an organization or department of that organization based on your analysis. It would therefore be useful to that organization to have those recommendations as a discrete part of your dissertation and it may be a course requirement. If you are making recommendations, you should consider who might carry out those recommendations and they must be actionable. MBA and DMS students are sometimes criticized for making vague and unfeasible recommendations; do not let this happen to you. If you have been researching a sector or a more general management issue, you may have found some implications for the whole sector. These may be broader and may take on a strategic rather than operational tone, but could be worth writing up as a separate element.

Conclusions

A strong finish to your dissertation is important whether or not the outcome of your research is world-changing. In your conclusions, you need to revisit the introduction and the research objectives. If your title was in the form of a question, have you actually answered it? You need to decide whether what you aimed to do when you started was what you actually did. As the process of research is circular, you need to complete the circle by returning to the beginning of your dissertation. You need to be explicit and state whether you met your research objectives and answered your research questions. Did you meet all or some of them, or some only partially? It does not really matter whether you met all your original objectives or just some of them, but it is important that you acknowledge the extent to which they have been achieved. If you found you have met some slightly different objectives, now is the time to change them retrospectively, but remember the examiners will be looking for consistency of purpose and this may have a knock-on effect elsewhere in the dissertation.

Your conclusion can suggest areas of further research on related themes or suggestions as to where the framework that you have created could be tested, perhaps in another sector. By doing this, you are showing an awareness of the evolutionary nature of research and offering either yourself or another researcher a basis for another project. It may be that you have found something at Masters' level that you wish to investigate further at PhD or DBA level. This chapter is the 'academic' end of your dissertation. It may be combined with the recommendations chapter.

Other uses for your dissertation

Having completed the writing up of your dissertation, you should congratulate yourself. Once you have drawn breath, you should consider whether there might be other destinations for your hard work. Masters' students often use their dissertations to enhance their employment prospects. Successful MBA and DMS graduates can seek promotion or change career paths using their dissertation as evidence of specialist knowledge. An MBA dissertation when rewritten as a consultancy project may be lucrative financially or it may create opportunities to do further projects within the chosen sector as a consultant. MSc and MA students can use their dissertations to improve their chances to start on their chosen graduate career path. Although no one is likely to be in a position to look at it at interview, the dissertation is evidence of what you are capable of.

Good quality Masters' dissertations with a rigorous methods chapter can be turned into conference papers or even an academic journal article if supported by your supervisor; indeed they might suggest this. A conference paper or academic journal article will involve additional work, but it does add credibility to your profile and will enhance your CV (resumé) if your research gets published.

Summary

This chapter has concentrated on the structure and presentation of your final written dissertation submission. Advice has been given on considering who the audience may be, how to construct logical written argument to support your work and how to make the best of all your hard work.

Suggested Activity

Even if you are not required to present your finished dissertation, it is a good idea to be able to present it verbally to a stranger. Plan a 3-minute mini-presentation about your project, its aims, context, methods, findings and conclusions on paper or using Microsoft PowerPoint®. This will help you cut out any extra 'padding' and assist you in being able to explain your research quickly and effectively to a non-expert audience, whether at a party, job interview or conference.

Discussion Questions

1   What criteria do you think Masters' examiners use when marking a dissertation?

2   Are there other uses for your Masters' dissertation? Who else might gain insight from reading it?

Further Reading

Jankowicz, A.D. (2000) *Business Research Projects* **(3rd edition). London: Business Press, Thomson Learning.** This contains some useful and practical advice on writing up.

References

Alvesson, M. and Willmott, H. (eds) (1992) *Critical Management Studies*. London: Sage.

Ansoff, I. (1972) *Corporate Strategy.* Middlesex: Penguin.

Armstrong, Michael (2003) *A Handbook of Human Resource Management Practice.* (9th edition). London: Kogan Page.

Astley, W. and Zummuto, R. (1992) 'Organisational science, managers and language games', *Organisational Science*, 3(4): 443–59.

Bailin, S., Case, R., Coombs, J.R., Daniels, L.B. (1999) 'Common misconceptions of critical thinking', *Journal of Curriculum Studies*, 31(3): 269–83.

Barclay, J. (1996) 'Learning from experience with learning logs', *Journal of Management Development*, 15(6): 28–44.

Bayley, G. and Nancarrow, C. (1998) 'Impulse purchasing: A qualitative exploration of the phenomenon', *Qualitative Market Research: An International Journal*, 1(2): Dove 99–114.

Bessant, J., Birley, S., Cooper, C., Dawson, S., Gennard, J., Gardiner, M., Gray, A., Jones, P., Mayer, C., McGee, J., Pidd, M., Rowley, G., Saunders, J. and Stark, A. (2003) 'The state of the field in UK management research: Reflections of the Research Assessment Exercise (RAE) panel', *British Journal of Management*, 14(1): 51–68.

Bloom, B.S., Engelhart, M.D., Furst, E.J., Hill, W.H. and Krathwohl, D.R. (1956) *Taxonomy of Education Objectives, Handbook I: Cognitive Domain*. New York: David McKay.

Bradley, F. (1991) *International Marketing Strategy*. London: Prentice Hall International.

Brassington, F. and Pettitt, S. (2003) *Principles of Marketing*. Harlow: FT Prentice Hall.

British Journal of Management (2001) 'Special issue: The nature of management research', 12(51).

Brown, S. (1995) 'Life begins at 40? Further thoughts on marketing's mid-life crisis', *Marketing Intelligence and Planning*, 13(1): 4–17.

Browne, M.N. and Freeman, K. (2000) 'Distinguishing features of critical thinking classrooms', *Teaching in Higher Education*, 5(3): 301–9.

Bryman, A. and Bell, E. (2003) *Business Research Methods*. Oxford: Oxford University Press.

Burgoyne, J. (1994) 'Managing by learning', *Management Learning,* 25(1): 35–55.

Buzan, Tony (1988[1977]) *Make the Most of your Mind*. London: Pan.

Christensen, R. (1981) 'Dear Diary: A learning tool for adults', *Lifelong Learning in the Adult Years*, October: 4–6.

Clarke, J. (2000) 'Tourism brands: An exploratory study of the brands box model', *Journal of Vacation Marketing*, 6(4): 329–45.

Coffey, A., Holbrook, B. and Atkinson, P. (1996) 'Qualitative data analysis: Technologies and representations', *Sociological Research Online*, 1(1). Available from: www.socresonline.org.uk/socresonline/1/1/4.html.

Collis, J. and Hussey, R. (2003) *Business Research: A Practical Guide* (2nd edition). Basingstoke: Palgrave Macmillan.

Cooper, D.R. and Schindler, P.S. (2003) *Business Research Methods* (8th edition). New York: McGraw-Hill.

Cooper, H. (1998) *Synthesizing Research: A Guide for Literature Reviews* (3rd edition). Thousand Oaks, CA: Sage.

Cottrell, S. (2003) *Skills for Success: The Personal Development Planning Handbook*, Basingstoke: Palgrave MacMillan.

Creswell, J.W. (2003) *Research Design: Qualitative, Quantitative, and Mixed Methods Approaches* (2nd edition). London: Sage.

Crix, J. (2004) *The Foundations of Research.* Basingstoke: Palgrave Macmillan.

Currie, G. and Knights, D. (2003) 'Reflecting on critical pedagogy in MBA education', *Management Learning*, 34(1): 27–49.

Das, T. (2003) 'Managerial perceptions and the essence of the managerial world: What is an interloper business executive to make of the academic research perceptions of managers?' *British Journal of Management*, 14: 23–32.

Dearing Report (1997) The National Committee of Inquiry into Higher Education. HMSO: The Learning Society.

De Bono, Edward (1977) *Lateral Thinking: A Textbook of Creativity*. London: Penguin.

De Chernatony, L. and McWilliam, G. (1989) 'The strategic implications of clarifying how marketers interpret brands', *Journal of Marketing Management*, 5(2): 153–71.

De Chernatony, L. and McWilliam, G. (1990) 'Appreciating brands as assets through using a two-dimensional model', *International Journal of Advertising*, 9: 111–19.

De Vaus, D.A. (2001) *Research Design in Social Research*. London: Sage.

De Vita, G. and Case, P. (2003) 'Rethinking the internationalisation agenda in UK higher education', *Journal of Further and Higher Education*, 27(4): 383–98.

Department of Trade and Industry (1998) *Our Competitive Future – Building the Knowledge-based Economy*, White Paper on competitiveness. London: DTI.

Du Boulay, D. (1999) 'Argument in reading: What does it involve and how can students become better critical readers?' *Teaching in Higher Education*, 4(2):147–63.

Ehrensal, K. (n.d.) 'Critical management studies and American business school culture'. Available from: www.mngt.waikato.ac.nz/ejrot/cmsconference/documents/Management%20Education/K_Ehrensal_CMS_paper.pdf. Accessed 14 September 2005.

Fisher, C. (2004) *Researching and Writing a Dissertation for Business Students*. Harlow: FT Prentice Hall.

Gibbs, G. (1988) *Learning by Doing: A Guide*. Birmingham: SCED.

Gilbert, J. (1993) 'Faster! Newer! Is not a strategy', *SAM Advanced Management Journal*, 58(2): 63–75.

Girden, E. (1996) *Evaluating Research Articles from Start to Finish*. Thousand Oaks, CA: Sage.

Guba, E.G. and Lincoln, Y.S. (1994) 'Competing paradigms in qualitative research', in N.K. Denzin and Y.S. Lincoln (eds) *Handbook of Qualitative Research*. Thousand Oaks, CA: Sage, pp. 105–17.

Gummesson, E. (1991) *Qualitative Methods in Management Research*. Thousand Oaks, CA: Sage.

Hammersley, M. (1992) *What's Wrong with Ethnography?* London: Routledge.

Hart, C. (1998) *Doing a Literature Review: Releasing the Social Science Research Imagination*. London: Sage.

Hassard, J. and Kelemen, M. (2002) 'Production and consumption in organisational knowledge: The case of the paradigms debate', *Organization*, 9(2): 331–55.

Hatchuel, A. (2001) 'The two pillars of new management research', *British Journal of Management*, 12 (special issue): S33–S39.

Hodgkinson, G.P., Herriot, P. and Anderson, N. (2001) 'Re-aligning the stakeholders in management research: Lessons from industrial, work and organizational psychology,' *British Journal of Management*, 12 (special issue): S41–S48.

Hofstede, G. (1984) *Culture's Consequences*. Beverley Hills, CA: Sage.

Hofstede, G. (2002) 'Dimensions do not exist: A reply to Brendan McSweeney', *Human Relations*, 55(11): 1355–62.

Johnson, G., Scholes, K. and Whittington, R. (2005) *Exploring Corporate Strategy* (7th edition). Harlow: FT Prentice Hall.

Kapferer, J-N. (2004) *The New Strategic Brand Management*. London: Kogan Page.

Keleman, M. and Bansal, P. (2002) 'The conventions of management research and their relevance to management practice', *British Journal of Management*, 13: 97–108.

Koch, A. (2001) 'Selecting overseas markets and entry modes: Two decision processes or one'? *Marketing Intelligence and Planning*, 19(1): 65–75.

Krueger, R.A. and Casey, M.A. (2000) *Focus Groups: A Practical Guide for Applied Research*. Thousand Oaks, CA: Sage.

Kuhn, T.S. (1962) *The Structure of Scientific Revolutions*. Chicago: University of Chicago Press.

LeCompte, M. and Goetz, J. (1982) 'Problems of reliability and validity in ethnographic research', *Review of Educational Research*, 52: 31–60.

Levitt, T. (1960) 'Marketing myopia', *Harvard Business Review*, 38(4): 45–56.

Lincoln, Y.S. and Guba, E.G. (1985) *Naturalistic Inquiry*. Thousand Oaks, CA: Sage.

Llewellyn, S. (2003) 'What counts as theory in qualitative management and accounting research?' *Accounting, Auditing and Accountability Journal*: 16(4): 662–708.

Martin, C.A. and Bush, A.J. (2000) 'Do role models influence teenagers' purchase intentions and behaviour?', *Journal of Consumer Marketing*, 17(5): 441–54.

McGivern, Y. (2003) *The Practice of Market Research: An Introduction*. Harlow: FT Prentice Hall.

McLaughlin, H. and Thorpe, R. (2000) 'All in vain: Lost voices in the development of management research', Management and Business Working Paper no WP00/04, Graduate Business School, Manchester Metropolitan University.

McSweeney, B. (2002a) 'Hofstede's model of national cultural differences and their consequences: A triumph of faith – a failure of analysis', *Human Relations*, 55(1): 89–128.

McSweeney, B. (2002b) 'The essentials of scholarship: A reply to Gert Hofstede', *Human Relations*, 55(11): 1363–72.

Metcalfe M. (2003) 'How to critique articles or presentations'. Unpublished paper, University of South Australia, Adelaide.

Mingers, J. (2000) 'What is it to be critical? Teaching a critical approach to management undergraduates', *Management Learning*, 31(2): 219–37.

Mintzberg, H. (1973) *The Nature of Managerial Work*. New York: Harper and Row.

Mintzberg, H. (2004) *Managers not MBAs: A Hard Look at the Soft Practice of Managing and Management Development*. London: FT Prentice Hall.

Miyauchi, Y. and Perry, C. (1999) 'Marketing fresh fruit to Japanese consumers: Exploring issues for Australian exporters', *European Journal of Marketing*, 33(1/2): 196–205.

Moon, J.A. (1999) *Reflection in Learning and Professional Development, Theory and Practice*. London: Kogan Page.

Moon, J.A. (2002) *Learning Journals: A Handbook for Academics, Students and Professional Development*. London: Kogan Page.

Mullins, L.J. (1999) *Management and Organisational Behaviour*. (5th edition) London: FT Pitman.

Norman, R. (1970) *A Personal Quest for Methodology*. Stockholm: Scandinavian Institutes for Administrative Research.

O' Dochartaigh, N. (2003) *The Internet Research Handbook*. London: Sage.

Peters, T.J. and Waterman, G. (1982) *In Search of Excellence*. New York: Harper and Row.

Pfeffer, J. (1993) 'Barriers to the advance of organisational science: Paradigm development as a dependent variable', *Academy of Management Review*, 18(4): 599–620.

Podsakoff, P.M. and Dalton, D.R. (1987) 'Research methodology in organizational studies', *Journal of Management*,13: 419–44.

Porter, M. (1971) *Competitive Strategy*. New York: The Free Press.

Porter, M. (1980) *Competitive Advantage*. New York: The Free Press.

Poulson, L. and Wallace, M. (eds) (2004) *Learning to Read Critically in Teaching and Learning*. London: Sage.

Priem, R.L. and Butler, J.E. (2001) 'Is the resource-based "view" a useful perspective for strategic management research?' *Academy of Management Review*, 26(1): 22–40.

Punch, K. (2000) *Developing Effective Research Proposals*. London: Sage.

QAA (2002) *QAA Subject Benchmarks for Masters Awards in Business and Management*. London: Association of Business Schools. Available from: www.the-abs.org.uk/QAA_masters_benchmark.pdf.

Quinton, S. and Smallbone, T. (2005) 'The troublesome triplets: Issues in teaching reliability, validity and generalisation to business students', *Teaching in Higher Education*, 10(3): 299–311.

Raimond, P. (1993) *Management Projects: Design, Research and Presentation*. London: Chapman and Hall.

Raju, P.S. (1995) 'Consumer behaviour in global markets: The A–B–C–D paradigm and its application to Eastern Europe and the Third World', *Journal of Consumer Marketing*, 12(5): 37–56.

Ramsden, P. (1992) *Learning to Teach in Higher Education*. London: Routledge.

Saunders, M.N.K., Lewis, P. and Thornhill, A. (2003) *Research Methods for Business Students* (3rd edition). Harlow: FT Prentice Hall.

Schofield, J.W. (1990) 'Increasing the generalizability of qualitative research', in R. Gomm, M. Hammersley and P. Foster (eds) (2000) *Case Study Method*. London: Sage, pp. 69–97.

Schön, D. (1983) *The Reflective Practitioner*. San Francisco: Josey-Bass.

Shoham, A. and Dalakas, V. (2003) 'Family consumer decision making in Israel: The role of teens and parents', *Journal of Consumer Marketing*, 20(3): 238–51.

Silverman, D. (1969) 'Correspondence: Organisation: A rejoinder', *Sociology*, 3(3): 420–1.

Shorter Oxford Dictionary (1993). Oxford: Oxford University Press.

Smallbone, T. and Quinton, S. (2004) 'Critical reading: Developing an approach to deep learning'. Paper presented to the Insititue of Teaching and Learning Conference, University of Hertfordshire, 30 June.

Stake, R. (1978) in N.K. Denzin and Y.S. Lincoln (eds) (1994) *Handbook of Qualitative Research*. Thousand Oaks, CA: Sage.

Starkey, K. and Madan, P. (2001) 'Bridging the relevance gap: Aligning stakeholders in the future of management research', *British Journal of Management*, 12 (special issue): S3–S26.

Sturdy, A. and Gabriel, Y. (2000) 'Missionaries, mercenaries or car salesmen? MBA teaching in Malaysia', *Journal of Management Studies*, 37(7): 979–1002.

Thietart, R.-A.,et al. (2001) *Doing Management Research*, translated by S. Wauchope. London: Sage.

Toulmin, S. (1958) *The Uses of Argument*. Cambridge: Cambridge University Press. Available from: www.willamette.edu/cla/rhetoric/courses/argumentation/Toulmin.htm.

Toyne, B. and Walters, P. (1989) *Global Marketing Management: A Strategic Perspective*. London: Allyn and Bacon.

Tranfield, D. and Starkey, K. (1998) 'The nature, social organization and promotion of management research: Towards policy', *British Journal of Management*, 9: 341–53.

Tranfield, D., Denyer, D., Marcos, J. and Burr, M. (2004) 'Co-producing management knowledge', *Management Decision*, 42(3/4): 375–86.

Vogt, W. (1993) *Dictionary of Statistics and Methodology*. Newbury Park, CA. Sage.

Walker, D. (1985) 'Writing and reflection', in D. Boud, R. Keogh and D. Walker (eds) *Reflection: Turning Experience into Learning*. London: Kogan Page, pp. 52–68.

Weaver, G.R. and Gioia, D.A. (1994) 'Paradigms lost: Incommensurability vs structurationist inquiry', *Organizational Studies*, 15(4): 565–90.

Wensley, R. (1997) 'Explaining success: The rule of ten percent and the example of market share', *Business Strategy Review*, 8(1): 63–70.

Wicks, A.C. and Freeman, R.E. (1998) 'Organisational studies and the new pragmatism: Positivism, anti-positivism and the search for ethics', *Organizational Science*, 9(2): 123–40.

Wilkinson, D. (1997) *Multiple Intelligence Theory and Teaching*, Oxford: OCSLD, Oxford Brookes University,

Williamson, O. (1985) *The Economic Institutions of Capitalism*. New York: The Free Press.

Willmott, H. (1994) 'Management education: Provocations to a debate', *Management Learning,* 25(1): 105–36.

Yin, R.K. (2003) *Case Study Research Design and Methods* (3rd edition). Thousand Oaks, CA: Sage.

Index

Added to a page number, 'f' denotes a figure.

abstracts
   dissertation structure 152–3
   journal articles 83
academic sources
   reliable web-based 74
   see also libraries
academics, collaboration between practitioners
      and 9–10
access, getting 53–4
acknowledgements, information sources 25
action plan framework, reflective journals 114, 121
activities, as basis for research topic 32–3
advocacy sites 75
AllSearch Engines 72
analysis
   of arguments 18–19
      journal articles 90–1
   dissertation structure 158–9
   secondary data 100–1
appraisal 20–7
appraise, definition 21
arguments
   analysis of 18–19
      journal articles 90–1
   presenting effective 145–6
   stages in constructing 146–7
assignments
   advantages of using secondary data 68–9
   note-taking for 23–4
audience, research 141–3
audio tapes, organizing 104–5
auditing process 135
authenticity 135
authority, critique of 21
authors
   debates/disagreements as research
         topics 34
   demonstrating knowledge of 56
   filing data by 103
   standing, journal articles 85

back-ups, data 104
background information
   in dissertations 154
   in research proposals 55
backing, of an argument 19

Bain Report (1994) 2
bias
   journal articles 136
   secondary data 69
bibliographic records 101–3
BIDS 72
books, secondary data 70–1
box files 103
brainstorming
   learning maps 45, 46f
   for research topics 28–9
browsing, for research topics 29
business
   critical thinking in 20
   databases, secondary data 72–4
   opportunities for research 12
   websites 75–6
Business Insight 72
business schools, management research 3–4
Business Source Premier 72, 75

CAQDAS 106
card index systems 102
career goals, as guide to research topics 32
case studies
   analysis 8
   generalization 133–4
catalytic authenticity 135
categorization, secondary data 99–100
claims, in arguments 19
classic funnel 148
classic model, argument construction 146–7
closed questions, coding 105
coding data 105–7
collaboration, academics and practitioners 9–10
commercial sources 77
community work, as basis for research topic 31
company sources 77
comparison, as basis for research topics 34
concepts, combining 150–1
conceptual journal articles, as source for
         research topics 34
conceptual tools 7
conclusions, in dissertations 159–60
concurrent validity 128
confirmability 135

constraints, describing in research proposals 57
construct validity 128
consultancy reports, audience 141–2
content validity 128
contextualization, of practical arguments 19
country information, in dissertations 154
coursework, building on, as research topic 29–30
creation, learning maps 38
creative problem-solving 39
credibility 135, 136
criterion-related validity 128
critical, definition 21
critical approach 15–27
    appraisal 20–7
    defined 15–16
    in higher education 16–20
    in management research 7–8
critical reading 22–3
critical self-awareness 134
critical theory, literature 8
critical thinking 16, 19–20
critical writing 147–52
criticism, definition 21
critique 8, 21
cross-analyses 131
cultural bias, journal articles 91
currency, of sources 85, 137

data
    coding 105–7
    organizing, worked example 108
    recording and cataloguing 101–3
    saving 104
    storing 103–4
    see also primary data; secondary data
data collection
    secondary data 98–101
    when to stop 97–8
data sticks 104
databases, secondary data 72–4
Dearing report (1997) 111
deductive method 6
degree level, management education 3
dependability 135
descriptiveness, of management research 9
dialectical approach, argument construction 146
directional hypotheses 51
discussion chapters, in dissertations 158–9
dissertations
    advantages of using secondary data 68–9
    audience 141–3
    constructing arguments 146–7
    critical writing 147–52
    incorporating reflection into 118–19
    other uses for 160
    planning 143–6
    reflection after completing 123–4
    as a source for research topics 33

dissertations cont.
    structure 152–60
    vivas and presentations 152
    see also research projects; research topics
DMS programmes 11–12, 13, 48
documentary data 67
dyslexic students, learning maps 24

EBSCO 72
EconLit 72
educative authenticity 135
electronic data storage 104
electronic referencing systems 102
Emerald 72, 73–4
EndNote 102
English, writing in 144
entertainment websites 76
entrepreneurship, research opportunities 12
errors, coding 106–7
ethics, describing in research proposals 57
Euromonitor 72
evolutionary process, reason for doing
    research 4–5
executive summaries 152–3
experimental designs, validity 127–8
exploratory research, generalization 132–3
external data sources 68
external pressures, to undertake
    research 5
external validity 129

face validity see internal validity
fairness 135
family, suggestions for research topics 32
feedback
    example of reflection on 123
    from teachers 121
filing systems 103
filtering, secondary data 98–9
finance, research opportunities 12
findings, in dissertations 158–9
floppy disks 104
force field analysis 39–40
Frankfurt School 21
friends, suggestions for research topics 32

generalizability 129, 134
generalization 132–4
Google 72
government sources 77
government websites 74–5
grand theory 7
grounds, of an argument 19

Harvard Business School 8
higher education, critical approach
    in 16–20
Hindu educational tradition 17

horizontal time line 150f
hypotheses 51–3

ideas
    openness to other 16
    relating to research topics 35
implications chapters, in dissertations 159
indexing, data 102
inductive approach 6, 128
industrial work, academic studies 10
inference 18
informal methods, quantifying data 100–1
information sources, acknowledging 25
information systems, opportunities for
        research 13
insight 8
inter-subjectivity 134
interests, as source for research
        topics 32–3
internal data sources 68
internal pressures, to undertake research 4
internal validity 126–8
Internet
    secondary data 71–2
    see also web-based resources
interpretivism 17
interviews, transcribing 105
introductions, in dissertations 153–4
inverted funnel 148–9
Investext 73

journal articles
    analysis 90–1
    asking questions 85–6
    critiquing style 89–90
    data storage 103–4
    framework for deconstructing 87–8
        practical worked example 93–5
    how to read 83–5
    note-taking from 25
    ontological perspectives 86–9
    reasons for reading 81–3
    reflecting on 91–2
    secondary data 71
    as a source for research topics 33–5
    web-based resources 74
journal databases, secondary data 72
journals, reflective *see* reflective journals
judgements, reflective 110
justification, role in argument 18

knowledge co-production 9–10
Koran, questioning approach 17
Kronbach's alpha 130

learning maps 38–9
    brainstorming 45, 46f
    included as appendices 44–5

learning maps *cont.*
    learning how to draw 40, 41f
    note-taking 24
learning processes 4
libraries
    browsing for research topics 29
    secondary data 70–1
    see also books; databases; journal articles;
        web-based resources
literature reviews
    critical writing 147–52
    in dissertations 154–6
lonesome pine 149, 150f

MA programmes 11–12, 13
management
    critical thinking in 20
    decisions, basis of 9
    issues, as basis for research topics 33
    knowledge, need to develop 9
    research opportunities 12
    as social phenomenon 8
management education
    critical approach 21
    degree level 3
management research 1–14
    in business schools 3–4
    contribution at postgraduate level 11–12
    contribution to theory 7
    critical approach 7–8
    defined 1–3
    disciplinary position 5
    expectations of 10–11
    nature and relevance 2
    opportunities for 12
    paradigms 5–6
    practitioners' view 9–10
    quality 2
    reasons for 4–5
    where to begin 12–13
management theory, defined 7
markers 142
marketing
    research 12
    as research topic 30
    websites 75–6
marking criteria 143
master reference files 102–3
MBA programmes 3, 4, 11–12, 13, 48
media sources 77
methods
    chapters, in dissertations 156–8
    outlining in research proposals 56
Microsoft Access 102
mind maps *see* learning maps
Mintel 72–3
modal qualifiers 19
modification, learning maps 38

MSc programmes 11–12, 13
multidisciplinary approach 3, 6
multiple paradigms, versus single 17–18
multiple source data 68

news documents, web-based 75
newspaper databases 73
non-directional hypotheses 51
normative theories, of management 3
note-taking 23–5
  plagiarism in 26–7
  using quotations 25–6
null hypotheses 51
numerical data, electronic storage 104
NVivo 106

objectivity, critique of 21
observation notes, transcribing 105
official documents, web-based resources 74–5
ontological authenticity 135
ontological perspective 6
open questions, coding 105–6
openness 7–8, 16
organizational psychology, academic
    studies 10
organizational research, approaches
    to 17–18

paradigm shifts 17
paradigms
  defined 5–6
  use of single versus multiple 17–18
patching 26
pedagogic strategies 4
peer auditing 135
peer review, academic journals 82–3
penalties, for plagiarism 27
personal development plans (PDPs) 120–1
personal web pages 76
perspectives
  choosing 13
  ontological 6
phenomenological approach 6, 7
plagiarism 26–7
planning, dissertations 143–6
plastic storage boxes 103
plausibility 136
pluralism 8
positioning statements 45–7
positivism 17, 18
  see also quantitative research
post-positivism 17
postgraduate research, contribution
    of 11–12
practice
  reflective 112
  see also professional practice
practitioner sources 77

practitioners
  reflective 120
  view, management research 9–10
pragmatic approach, paradigm choice 18
predictive validity 128
presentation 142–3, 152
press releases, government 74
primary data
  getting access 53
  journal articles, analysis 87–8, 91
  organizing 104–5
problem-solving, creative 39
professional practice, reflective journals as
    an aid to 119–20
PROMT 73
Proquest 73

qualitative data, coding 106
qualitative research 6
  external validity 129
  internal validity 128
  plausibility and credibility 136
  reliability 129–30, 135
quality, of management research 2
quantifying data 100–1
quantitative research 6
  external validity 129
  internal validity 127
  reliability 130
  US business schools 3
questioning
  as foundation of critical approach 17, 20
  journal articles 85–6, 91–2
  see also research questions
quotations, using 25–6

reading
  critical 22–3
  journal articles *see* journal articles
rebuttal, of an argument 19
recommendations, in dissertations 159
recording
  data 101–4
  reflections 112–14
Reference Manager 102
references
  in journal articles, checking 84
  in research proposals 58
  to academic journals 81, 82
  to websites 77
referencing systems 102–3
reflection 110–24
  after completing dissertations 123–4
  defined 110
  getting started 111–14
  importance of learning 111
  incorporating into dissertations 118–19
  journal articles 91–2

reflection-in-action 111
reflection-on-action 111–12
reflective journals
  as an aid to professional practice 119–20
  practical worked examples 115, 122–3
  privacy 116
  using in research 116–17
  when to write 116
  writing 113
    format 115–16
    framework for 114–15
reflective practitioners 120
reflexive understanding 4
relationships, hypothesis testing 51
reliability 129–32
repetition, evaluating validity 134
research objectives 49–50
  listing 47–8
  practical worked example 50
  research proposal statements 55
research projects 44–66
  establishing boundaries 44–5
  getting access 53–4
  hypotheses 51–3
  positioning statements 45–7
  research objectives 49–50
    listing 47–8
  research questions 48–9
    listing 47–8
  time management 54
  writing research proposals 54–65
research proposals 54–65
  MSc presentation example 58–60
  practical worked example 60–5
  review of academic literature 56–8
  suggested content 55
research questions 48–9
  listing 47–8
  research proposal statements 55
  see also questioning
research topics 28–43
  checklist for feasible 35–6
  ideas, developing and mapping 37–41
  objectives, questions and hypotheses,
    developing 47
  practical worked example 36–7
  techniques and tools for finding 28–35
researchers, self-critical 16
resources, in research proposals 57
rhetoric, critique of 21

samples 136
saving data 104
science of administration 3
search engines 72
secondary data 67–80
  advantages of using 68–9
  data collection

secondary data cont.
  categorization 99–100
  filtering 98–9
  knowing the right place to look 76–7
  preparing for analysis 100–1
  where to start 69–71
  where to go next 71–4
  when to stop looking 77–8
  demonstrating breadth of sources 76–7
  practical worked example 78–9
  source categories 77
  types of 67–9
  web-based resources
    checklist for evaluating 79–80
    reliable 74–6
sector information, in dissertations 154
self-awareness, critical 134
self-critical researchers 16
single paradigms, versus multiple 17–18
small and medium sized enterprises (SMEs),
    research opportunities 12
social phenomenon, management as 8
social sciences, management's position in 3
softer research methods 4
software, for coding data 106
SOSIG 72
specialist knowledge, as basis for research
    topic 32–3
spider diagrams see learning maps
split-half correlations 130
statements, key research questions and
    objectives 55
storing data 103–4
structure, dissertations 152–60
style
  journal articles 89–90
  research writing 10
summaries, of note-taking 25
summary sheets, data records 105
survey data 67–8
SWOT analysis 121
synthesis
  learning maps 38
  theory and practice 82

tables, note-taking in 24–5
tactical authenticity 135
test-re-test 130
textbooks
  datedness of 81
  as source for research topics
    30–1, 36–7
themes
  analysis of data 101
  linked 151
theoretical congruence 135
theoretical journal articles, analysis of 91
theorizing, five levels of 7

theory and practice
  gap between 4, 8
  synthesis 82
  see also management theory;
    Vedic theory
theory testing, as research topic 34–5
theses, as a source for research topics 33
thinking
  classification of levels 50
  critical 16, 19–20
Thomson Gale 73
time lines 149–50
time management
  describing in research proposals 57
  research projects 54
titles
  journal articles 83
  see also working titles
tourism research 12
trade press 75
tradition, critique of 21
transcription, interviews and observation
    notes 105
transdisciplinary approach 3
transferability 135
transformation 8
triangulation 131, 132f
trustworthiness 135

understanding
  improvement through research 4
  reflexive 4
United States, management research in 3
units of analysis, coding data 107

universities
  management research in 2
  pressures to undertake research 4, 5
  websites 76

validity 126–9
  alternative criteria to evaluate 134–6
Vedic theory 17
Venn diagrams 45
verbs, to describe research objectives 49–50
verisimilitude 135
video tapes, organizing 104–5
vivas 152
voluntary work, as research topic 31

warrant, of an argument 19
web-based resources
  bibliographic records 102
  checklist for evaluating 79–80
  reliable 74–6
  searching for 76
WebFetch 72
work experience, as research topic 31
working titles 55
workplace, reflection 111–12
writing
  critical 147–52
  hypotheses 51
  listing questions and objectives 47–8
  reflective journals *see* reflective journals
    research proposals 54–65
  style of 10

Zetoc 72